REAL ESTATE ISSUES IN THE HEALTH CARE INDUSTRY

Current Topics in Real Estate
Finance and Economics

Editors:

James B. Kau
Department of Real Estate
University of Georgia
Athens, Georgia U.S.A.

C. F. Sirmans
Center for Real Estate and
Urban Economic Studies
University of Connecticut
Storrs, Connecticut U.S.A.

Other books in the series:

Chinloy, P.:
Real Estate: Investment and Financial Security

Durning, D.:
Mortgage Revenue Bonds

REAL ESTATE ISSUES IN THE HEALTH CARE INDUSTRY

Proceedings of the First Annual Conference
of the Health Care Real Estate Institute

edited by
Ronald S. Barak
and
Sherwin L. Memel

Co-Sponsored by

The University of Southern California
School of Business Administration
School of Public Administration
School of Urban & Regional Planning

Manatt Phelps & Phillips

USC

MANATT
PHELPS
PHILLIPS
ATTORNEYS AT LAW

WKAP ARCHIEF

Kluwer Academic Publishers
Boston/Dordrecht/London

Distributors for North America:
Kluwer Academic Publishers
101 Philip Drive
Assinippi Park
Norwell, Massachusetts 02061 USA

Distributors for all other countries:
Kluwer Academic Publishers Group
Distribution Centre
Post Office Box 322
3300 AH Dordrecht, THE NETHERLANDS

Library of Congress Cataloging-in-Publication Data

A C.I.P. Catalogue record for this book is available from the Library of Congress.

Printed on acid-free paper.

Printed in the United States of America

Table of Contents

ADVISORY COMMITTEE

PLANNING COMMITTEE

RONALD S. BARAK, Co-Chair

SHERWIN L. MEMEL, Co-Chair

Anthony J. Abbate
Senior Vice President,
Advocacy Services
Hospital Council of Southern California
Los Angeles, California

Gregory A. Adams
President/CEO
Saint Bernardine Medical Center
San Bernardino, California

Michael Bobrow
Design Principal
Bobrow/Thomas & Associates (BTA, Inc.)
Los Angeles, California

Peter E. Braveman
Vice President for Legal Affairs
Cedars-Sinai Medical Center
Los Angeles, California

Christine W. Brown
Director of Network Development
ScrippsHealth
San Diego, California

Jerry L. Buckingham
Former Administrator Facilities Implementation Team
Department of Health Services Los Angeles County
Los Angeles, California

Donald M. Cook
President and CEO
Donald Cook Associates, Inc.
San Marino, California

Judy Pierson Ellison
President
Quadrant Group, Inc.
Los Angeles, California

Christine R. Hall
General Counsel
California Association of Hospitals and Health Systems
Sacramento, California

Charles H. Harrison
Audit Partner
Arthur Anderson & Co.
Los Angeles, California

Kenneth A. Kneale
Real Estate Consultant
Blue Cross of California
Woodland Hills, California

Arron F. Latt
Vice President
Leonard Nadler Associates, Inc.
Los Angeles, California

Burt Margolin
Former Assemblyman
Los Angeles, California

Marc S. Margulis
Managing Director
Houlihan Lokey Howard & Zukin
Los Angeles, California

Craig L. McKnight
Partner
Coopers & Lybrand
Philadelphia, Pennsylvania

Ron J. Messenger
President and CEO
Paraceisus Healthcare Corporation
Pasadena, California

Dr. Robert C. Myrtle
Professor of Health Services Administration and Professor of Gerontology
School of Public Administration
University of Southern California
Los Angeles, California

Leonard Nadler
President
Leonard Nadler Associates, Inc.
Los Angeles, California

Edward Poll, Esq.
Edward Poll & Associates, Inc.
Venice, California

Philip R. Schimmel
Partner
KPMG Peat Marwick LLP
Long Beach, California

Barry P. Schochet
President and Chief Operating Officer, Hospital Division
National Medical Enterprises, Inc.
Santa Monica, California

Thomas R. Testman
Former Partner of Ernst & Young LLP
San Juan Capistrano, California

Julia Thomas
Chairman, President and CEO
Bobrow/Thomas & Associates (BTA, Inc.)
Los Angeles, California

Eric A. Tuckman
Vice President and General Counsel
Centinela Hospital Medical Center
Inglewood, California

PREFACE

Coupled with the general decline in real estate values and opportunities for capital formation, the health care industry is in the midst of unprecedented change that has resulted in unneeded real estate, excess debt and a major need for capital to meet new organizational challenges.

Indeed, these are challenging times, evolutionary if not revolutionary: Reorganizations. Restructures. Shakeouts. Closures.

Do you know what the strategic alternatives and solutions are for your facility or organization? Has your 1980s health care *asset* become a 1990s *liability?* What will your organization look like in the post-health care reform era, and how will your real estate help -- or hinder -- this transition?

If the private payor doesn't get you, the government may. If the government doesn't get you, the market will. Only the strong, the swift and the knowledgeable will survive these "winds of change" and the various forces at play today. Will your organization be one of those which do?

If you are unsure of the answers to these questions, this publication may be for you. Based upon the inaugural University of Southern California/Manatt Phelps Phillips **Health Care Industry Real Estate Institute**, held in Los Angeles, California on February 9, 1995, if this book does not provide all of the answers, it will provide some, as well as assisting the reader at least to identify the questions that need asking, and answering.

Los Angeles, California. January 1996.

Ronald S. Barak　　　　Sherwin L. Memel

PROGRAM OVERVIEW

9:00 a.m. **WELCOME**

Dr. Jane G. Pisano
Vice President for External Affairs
University of Southern California

Edward J. Blakely
Dean, School of Urban & Regional Planning

Dr. David Dale-Johnson
Chair, Real Estate Department
School of Business Administration

9:15 a.m. **INTRODUCTION**

Ronald S. Barak, Esq. (Co-Chair)
Chair, Real Estate Department
Manatt, Phelps & Phillips

Sherwin L. Memel, Esq. (Co-Chair)
Chair, Health Law Department
Manatt, Phelps & Phillips

9:30 a.m. **THE HEALTH CARE FACILITIES AUDIT**
HAS YOUR 1980s HEALTH CARE FACILITIES ASSET BECOME A 1990s LIABILITY?

Daniel M. Cain, President
Cain Brothers & Company, Incorporated
New York, NY

Michael Calhoun, Vice President
Lewin-VHI, Inc.
Corte Madera, CA

Michael D. Stephens, President & CEO
Hoag Memorial Hospital Presbyterian
Newport Beach, CA

Dr. R. Tarantello
Tarantello & Associates
Newport Beach, CA

10:15 a.m. **BREAK**

10:30 a.m. **IMPLEMENTING THE HEALTH CARE FACILITIES AUDIT**
THE HEALTH CARE FACILITIES AUDIT "MATRIX"

Michael Bobrow, Design Principal
Bobrow/Thomas and Associates (BTA, Inc.)
Los Angeles, CA

Judy Pierson Ellison, President
Quadrant Group, Inc.
Los Angeles, CA

Charles H. Harrison, Audit Partner
Arthur Andersen & Co.
Los Angeles, CA

Marc S. Margulis, Managing Director
Houlihan Lokey Howard & Zukin
Los Angeles, CA

12:00 **LUNCHEON**

Sandra R. Smoley, Secretary
California Health & Welfare Agency

1:30 p.m. **CAPITAL FORMATION IN THE 1990s**
RESTRUCTURES, WORKOUTS, REORGANIZATIONS

Simon Aron, Esq.
Manatt, Phelps & Phillips
Los Angeles, CA

Bryan P. Marsal, Managing Director
Alvarez & Marsal, Inc.
New York, NY

Craig L. McKnight, Partner
Coopers & Lybrand
Philadelphia, PA

Charles G. Plimpton, Vice President
John Nuveen & Co. Incorporated
Irvine, CA

Albert E. Smith, Senior Vice President
General Electric Capital Corporation
Dallas, TX

2:45 p.m. **BREAK**

3:00 p.m. **AFTERNOON WORKSHOPS**

A. THE HEALTH CARE FACILITIES AUDIT "MATRIX"
Moderators:

Michael Bobrow, Design Principal
Bobrow/Thomas and Associates (BTA, Inc.)
Los Angeles, CA

Judy Pierson Ellison, President
Quadrant Group, Inc.
Los Angeles, CA

Dr. R. Tarantello
Tarantello & Associates
Newport Beach, CA

Anthony Roesch, AIA
Bobrow/Thomas & Associates (BTA, Inc.)
Chicago, IL

B. REGULATORY IMPACT
Moderators:

Rick L. Grossman, Esq.
Manatt, Phelps & Phillips
Los Angeles, CA

Eric A. Tuckman, Esq.
Vice President & General Counsel
Centinela Hospital Medical Center
Inglewood, CA

C. PROJECTING OPERATIONS
Moderators:

Charles H. Harrison, Audit Partner
Arthur Andersen & Co.
Los Angeles, CA

Marc S. Margulis, Managing Director
Houlihan Lokey Howard & Zukin
Los Angeles, CA

D. CAPITAL FORMATION

Moderators:

Daniel M. Cain, President
Cain Brothers & Company, Incorporated
New York, NY

Charles G. Plimpton, Vice President
John Nuveen & Co. Incorporated
Irvine, CA

Albert E. Smith, Senior Vice President
General Electric Capital Corporation
Dallas, TX

E. RESTRUCTURES, WORKOUTS & REORGANIZATIONS

Moderators:

Simon Aron, Esq.
Manatt, Phelps & Phillips
Los Angeles, CA

Bryan P. Marsal, Managing Director
Alvarez & Marsal, Inc.
New York, NY

Craig L. McKnight, Partner
Coopers & Lybrand
Philadelphia, PA

3:45 p.m. **BREAK**

4:00 P.M. **THE EXPERTS SHOW YOU HOW TO DO IT: A CASE STUDY**

Gregory A. Adams, President/CEO
Saint Bernardine Medical Center
San Bernardino, CA

George H. Bristol, Director, Corporate Finance
Ernst & Young
Los Angeles, CA

Judy Pierson Ellison, President
Quadrant Group, Inc.
Los Angeles, CA

Rick L. Grossman, Esq.
Manatt, Phelps & Phillips
Los Angeles, CA

Nancy L. Milby, Partner
KPMG Peat Marwick LLP
Long Beach, CA

Jeffrey S. Pion, First Vice President
CB Commercial
Los Angeles, CA

Eric A. Tuckman, Esq.
Vice President & General Counsel
Centinela Hospital Medical Center
Inglewood, CA

5:00 p.m. **COCKTAIL RECEPTION FOR ALL PARTICIPANTS**

INTRODUCTION &

OPENING REMARKS

HEALTH CARE INDUSTRY REAL ESTATE INSTITUTE
FEBRUARY 9, 1995
Transcription of Seminar

EDWARD POLL: Welcome to the Health Care Industry Real Estate Institute seminar which is co-sponsored by the University of Southern California and the law firm of Manatt, Phelps & Phillips. We're excited to be with you today. We look forward to your involvement and participation with the panelists and speakers throughout the day. In order to facilitate the presentations, however, we ask you to hold your questions during the presentations of the individual speakers until the question and answer session at the end of each panel when we encourage your active participation.

You have before you a syllabus which you were given on the way in. Allow me to give you an overview of that syllabus. Each tab has the presentation for each panel, respectively. At the beginning of the afternoon session, I will give you an additional handout. This will be used for the fourth panel which is the case study. The case study panel will be a real live situation, one that we think you will be sure to walk away from with some important insights. At lunchtime, a special treat for us will be our keynote speaker, Sandra R. Smoley, Secretary of Health and Welfare Agency for the State of California.

At this time, it gives me a great deal of pleasure to introduce the representatives of our co-sponsor, the University of Southern California. The first to speak to us will be Jane Pisano. Dr. Pisano is the Dean of the School of Public Administration. Next will be Dr. Ed Blakely, who is the Dean of the School of Urban and Regional Planning. The third speaker will be David Dale-Johnson, who is the Director of the Program for Real Estate in the School of Business Administration. Please welcome our three co-sponsors. Dr. Pisano.

JANE G. PISANO: I am delighted to welcome you to this day. This conference is an exciting partnership between the University of Southern California and the Manatt law firm. When Sherwin Memel and Ed Poll first broached the idea of doing a session like this, I was immediately attracted to it, because I hold Sherwin Memel and Ed Poll in high regard. I don't need to tell you about all the changes that are happening in healthcare and in healthcare/real estate, particularly in hospitals. That's why we're here. This subject lends itself particularly well to a day like this, because it is complex: at the intersection of government regulation, public policy, business decisions and real estate. We cannot see the future yet we must think strategically anyway.

Today's program has been crafted so that you will get these multiple perspectives. It is our hope that you will find today's session of value as you think about critical real estate decisions for your company. Of course, we look forward to next year when we hope to sponsor the second conference.

EDWARD J. BLAKELY: Good morning, I'm glad to be here as well. This conference, I think, represents a nice merger, and we're all thinking mergers and acquisitions these days; a merger of the health professions and real estate professions. We are all struggling in difficult times to deal with changed circumstances. The changed circumstances are obviously markets. The markets have shifted in all of the real estate industry, and in terms of demographic changes, changes in peoples' tastes, preferences in mind, and globalization. I think this is a great opportunity between our professions to see what we can do together. This conference represents a whole new horizon in my perspective, because the conference suggests that you're going to audit, examine the matrix between what exactly is the real estate asset we have, and how it might be utilized. I want to show you the past, how I see it, and the future in real estate -- health real estate. This might prepare some of you right now to recognize this kind of a health facility, grand entrance ways, old technologies that some of you, who are as old as I am, remember, and not too appealing, the presentation.

But, health is changing, our plans are changing, we now have to serve multiple clients, provide total century care, and recognize the added value of the pieces of real estate. And some medical complexes have begun to do this. This is a medical complex in Ft. Worth, designed as a child care complex. Child-centered, most importantly, yet it's real estate centered, and that real estate can be used for other new and different purposes. The Robert Garner Center in Alberta, a mall hospital, added new value to the real estate, because this real estate is serving multiple purposes. Building single-purpose facilities may not be the right decision for the future of many kinds of real estate. There are new kinds of entrances that don't look like hospitals any more. As a matter of fact, these days, we really have to find the hospital entrance by looking at the sign, which is the hospital or the clinic. However, that's because these new facilities are valued as pieces of real estate. Both outside and inside. For instance, this is the inside of the University of California at San Diego and those are real palm trees.

We're serving clients in new and different ways. All of us in the real estate industry and the health industry have to recognize that we have to be more sophisticated in addressing those clients, and bringing new expertise to that business. That's what this conference is all about, bringing new tools to that enterprise. The Law Center and Real Estate Program at the University of Southern California are considering some health-care issues. I'm examining high technology and medical technology. We have others looking at hospitals and hospital configurations, and we're willing to serve you and your industry. Thank you very much.

DAVID DALE-JOHNSON: I am David Dale-Johnson, the Director of the Program in Real Estate in the Business School. Welcome. We're delighted to be partial sponsors of this program. I think we've prepared an innovative program, and we hope it will continue to grow. Ever since this conference became a collective glint in the planning committee's eyes, the healthcare landscape has changed dramatically, within a year and a half. Given the failure of the last Congress to pass sweeping healthcare reform, competition will clearly take a greater role as we move forward with the managed care system. Patients who want their demands met will be recognized and answered by the industry. Providers, as they develop and continue to enhance their corporate strategies, will be keeping this in mind. Had the Clinton Health Care plan survived, there would have been much more concern for average care, and I think the role of competition would have been much less important. As we move ahead, a key element of provider strategy must be delivery systems, where facilities and management of these facilities are consistent with that strategy. That's why all of you are here today.

Marketing and the role of place, location, amenity and services in these facilities, are going to be extremely important in order for service deliverers to compete, survive and be profitable. Again, we're delighted to be part of the sponsors, and we hope you enjoy the program.

POLL: Thank you, David. Some of the things we hope will come out of today are your reactions, your evaluations of not only this program, but the concept itself, and what we can do to better serve you in the next year, and the years to come. With that, let me turn the program over to Ron Barak, the Chair of the Real Estate Department of the law firm of Manatt, Phelps & Phillips, to begin the program. Thank you very much.

RONALD S. BARAK: Good morning. I'm Ron Barak. Along with my partner, Sherwin Memel, we'll be chairing these proceedings today. I'm basically a real estate transactions lawyer, but I sometimes have occasion to be involved in real estate related litigation, and to prepare witnesses for their deposition testimony. The first thing we typically say to a client when preparing them is "Keep your answers short. Listen to the question. If you can answer it with a `yes' or `no,' do so, and don't go any further. If somebody says `Do you know where you were on the night of June 12, 1994 at 10:15 in the evening,' your answer should be `yes' or `no.' The question wasn't `where were you.' Well, that seems pretty simple, and the first couple of times I gave someone instructions like that, they seemed to understand, and I thought that was all that was needed. But it never worked. So I changed the approach a little bit. I'd make the same speech, but then I'd also pull out my wallet and take out a $100 bill. (It's not that I generally have $100 bills in my wallet, but I was prepared.) I'd hand the client the $100 bill and I'd say, "Stick to this rule, follow it today and the $100 is yours." I haven't lost the $100 yet. On a few occasions, the client I was preparing for the deposition was a lawyer. Now, you think that would take less preparation. No, I've learned that when I'm doing this with a client who's a lawyer, you have to take out about five $100 bills. That's not because the $100 isn't important to them. It's because I haven't found a lawyer yet who doesn't just love to hear himself talk!

I'm going to try to be the exception. I'm going to make some brief comments and then turn the podium over to Sherwin to move us forward. The preliminary comments I want to offer are these: As chairman of Manatt, Phelps' Health Law Department, Sherwin's responsibility today will be to offer the perspective of the healthcare industry looking at its real estate. As chairman of Manatt, Phelps' Real Estate Department, I'm going to do just the reverse, look with somewhat of a hard eye at the healthcare industry from the perspective of the real estate community. The first observation I want to offer, which we'll test as the day progresses, is to say that as central as real estate is to the deployment of healthcare services, real estate, and real estate principles, on the one hand, and the healthcare industry, on the other hand, are, surprisingly, strangers to one another. Frankly, they seem to be somewhat uncomfortable with one another.

Historically, real estate was somewhat of a no-brainer, at least in comparison to real estate today. I think the healthcare industry had the luxury of approaching its real estate in that vein. Without much difficulty, the healthcare industry was able to control its real estate assets.

In the nineties, with the changes and challenges confronting the healthcare industry in particular, and the adverse market impact on real estate, this relationship has turned somewhat on its side. Today, healthcare real estate seems to be controlling the healthcare industry. This is not a good thing. It needs to be fixed. There are some in the healthcare industry who are genuinely starting to address this, but, I submit to you, there is much more to be done by many more, and the clock is running. With this caution, I place you in the capable hands of my partner and colleague, Sherwin Memel.

SHERWIN L. MEMEL: Thank you, Ron. As Ron said, I will bring the healthcare perspective to this symposium, and try to assist those here who are in the real estate arena, in understanding why healthcare real estate is unique, and cannot be looked at as you might look at an ordinary office building transaction or something of that sort. There is so much more at stake in a real estate situation and in analyzing it. I hope this program today helps those in the real estate arena to understand that.

In the United States, we have about plus or minus 6,000 hospitals, of which 1,000 are for-profit. However, the non-profit hospitals and the governmental hospitals are another piece of that sector. The largest number of those 6,000 hospitals that are not-for-profit, either religious or community not-for-profit hospitals, learned a long time ago that even though they are "not-for-profit," they must earn a bottom line in order to keep up with expanding technology, or they must replace plant and equipment in order that all healthcare providers are in a position of having some sort of a surplus at year-end. Now, prior to the evolutionary steps that have led us to where we are now, which began in the early eighties, the theory was *keep the beds full.* Keep the patients in the beds, do as many tests as you can, obviously, within the parameters of good medicine. The doctors wanted to see the patients as much as they could because it was fee for service, and the incentive structure was better. In 1982 and 1983 we began to see some radical changes in the status.

First, there was a change on both the federal level and the state level. There was a change on the state level, where the insurance companies did not have to permit patients to select any hospital or any physician they wanted. Selective contracting was established, where individual hospitals were in positions to be chosen. For example, as an insurance company we will deal with you, if you can be more effective in your pricing by keeping costs down. We were hearing the stories of how U.S. Steel, rather General Motors, was spending more money for healthcare per car for its workers than it was spending for steel going into the car. The employers were really starting to scream about escalating premiums. In addition, we began to see, at the federal level, prospective payment, diagnostic within groups, many illnesses categories, 460-some-odd categories of illness, and the government would pay for Medicare patients right away.

At that time, you were paid on a cost basis. Perhaps you were paid something above that, and the more costs you had, the more you were paid on a fee-for-service basis, and you were allowed to keep whatever you received. On this case basis, it was a flat amount, and if you kept people in longer, you would lose a lot of money.

As time went on, we began to see capitation creep more and more into this. Capitation, simply stated, is like the Kaiser system, where they will pay physicians, or increasingly, hospitals, so much per person per month. You get an employer group, they would put an amount, and they would give you so much per month to take care of the health of this entire population. Now, obviously, the less healthcare services you render, whether it's in the hospital or outside the hospital, the less tests you give, and the more you get to keep of that capitation amount. Therefore, the incentives, over the last twelve years or so, have been totally reversed. Now, the theory is, what do we need all this real estate for? We in California, for example, have an average occupancy of around 48%. Once upon a time, we could talk about 80% or 90% occupancies in hospitals.

We also have a situation where about 40 hospitals have closed in the last five years in California. Now, this is true throughout the United States. What we're seeing is a tremendous consolidation of resources, the growth of these giant companies, like Columbia, HCA, the giant health maintenance organizations, and the HMOs, which sell this capitated care. They are making huge returns -- 30% per year down to the bottom line, and somewhere around 65% of all workers in the major industrial corporations are being taken care of on these capitated plans. In California, about 75% of all privately insured people are under these capitated plans.

The way the federal government has paid physicians under Medicare has spread from the government programs into the private sectors. After decades and decades of being the king, our specialists have suddenly become the second-class citizens. Their incomes are plummeting like out-of-control elevators. The general practitioners and the primary care physicians are the gatekeepers. They decide who can and cannot go to specialists. They decide who can and cannot go to hospitals. That is because they want to keep more of this capitation amount. This is a consolidation of physician groups and of hospital organizations, which we'll hear more about today, and it is taking place because they want to sell cost-effective networks to the employer/payer arena, creating a limited situation for everyone.

Now, questions of quality arise. Questions of whether people are getting appropriate care, excess hospitalization, excess testing, excess medical visits, unnecessary surgeries, and all of the raps that were against the healthcare field in the fee-for-service sector, are now reversed. The questions are "I can't get my doctor to let me in the hospital, I can't get this test, he says my back doesn't need the surgery." And so on and so forth. Therefore, the monitoring of quality is a continuing problem. Nonetheless, all of this has now resulted in a shift in use. The payers are now recognizing that it is cheaper to pay for treatment on an outpatient basis, and they switched to do that a decade ago. Hence, care is being shifted to outpatient facilities. Care is also being shifted into the homes. Now, instead of one or two doctor offices, large groups are getting together in order to take these big capitation amounts. The medical office buildings, which were designed for one or two physician practices, are no longer fit for their purposes, and the hospitals all have this tremendous amount of surplus bed capacity. How do we deal with these challenges? That's what we hope today's program will ascertain. It is my pleasure to introduce the speakers who will be part of our first panel.

THE HEALTH CARE FACILITIES AUDIT

Has your 1980s Health Care Facilities Asset Become a 1990s Liability?

THE HEALTH CARE FACILITIES AUDIT

Has your 1980s Health Care Facility *Asset* Become a 1990s *Liability*?

In this Part I, we review:

□ **The Health Care Delivery "Evolution."** Over the past decade, how have we gotten to where we are today? Where are we today? Employer purchasing coalitions. Health insurance purchasing cooperatives. Where are we heading? Federal action. State action. Market forces.

□ **Development/Land Use and Health Care Regulation**. What "drove" this development in the past? Why are we at over capacity and/or obsolete today? How do licensing and related regulatory considerations (industry and facility) impact continued and/or alternative use?

□ **Declining Values and Capital Formation Opportunities, Excess Debt, Tax Constraints**. Impact of a declined, or declining, economy. Impact of declined, or declining, values. Impact of declined, or declining, revenues and/or profit margins. Impact of fixed long term taxable and tax-exempt debt. The limitations of single purpose facilities. Increasing demand for decreasing capital formation opportunities.

□ **The Alternatives**. Removal--cut your losses and run. Consolidation--improve your ratios. Cost cutting reduced to a fine art. Adapting to managed care pricing. Hanging in there while the competition drops out. Reconfiguration--go with the 1990s flow. Impact of HMOs, mergers, sales, exchanges of facilities, formation of giant for-profit and nonprofit hospital chains. Formation of networks of affiliated hospitals. Physician/hospital integration. Consolidation of physician groups. Insurance companies as major players.

Sherwin L. Memel, Esquire
Manatt, Phelps & Phillips
Los Angeles, CA

MEMEL: Rocky Tarantello is the Associate Professor of Real Estate and Economics at USC. He has a Doctorate of Business Administration and a Master of Business Administration from USC. Among his professional credentials are a certificate from the American Society of Real Estate Counselors. He's a full member of the Land Institute. He is President of TARANTELLO Associates, a California-BASED real estate counseling company, and he has tremendous experience in real estate development, and investment in hard research. He is an author. He has been an expert witness in many cases, and is a public speaker, who discusses and analyzes healthcare facility costs.

Dan Cain is a veteran in the healthcare finance field, and a founding partner and a principle of the CAIN Brothers. A widely recognized expert in healthcare finance, he has guided the CAIN Brothers with creativity and wisdom through 20 years of healthcare financing. Prior to the CAIN Brothers, he was an officer of Eastman Dillon healthcare funding, and began his early career at Merrill Lynch. He's a trustee of Universal Health and Income Trust. He has a New York Stock Exchange company, and he is a frequent speaker and author. He has an MBA in finance from Columbia University.

Michael Stevens has his Master's in Hospital Administration from Columbia University School of Public Health, and in Administrative Medicine. He also has his MBA. He, too, is a veteran of the healthcare wars. He is a past president of the California Association of Hospitals and Health Systems. He started his career early on in New York and went to the Greenville Hospital System. Since 1985 he has been an executive at Hoag Memorial Hospital Presbyterian in Newport Beach, California, one of the most prestigious hospitals in the

United States. He was the administrator from 1985 through 1994, and he has been president since December of 1994. He has served on the board, was on the board of Blue Cross of California, is a delegate to two recent policy boards of the American Hospital Association, and has an outstanding set of credentials.

Michael Calhoun is one of those over-achievers who is an outstanding scholar in international affairs, has belonged to the London School of Economics and the Woodrow Wilson School of Public Health and International Affairs at Princeton University, and also has a law degree from Harvard Law School.

I used to kid my partners by saying you could always tell a lawyer from Harvard, but you can't identify them that easily. Michael has conducted extensive research in healthcare, and he has written a book which will be coming out soon called, "Understanding Healthcare Reform in the United States." From 1989 to 1992 he was the Chief of Staff of the Department of Health and Human Services. In his earlier career, he was a member of the staff of the Committee on Ways and Means of the U.S. House of Representatives. He has practiced law at some prestigious law firms; he is vice-president; and heads the office of LEWIN-VHI for the west coast.

For those of you who haven't heard of the organization, it is probably the preeminent think-tank in the United States. It does constant studies for the U.S. government and state governments, as well as private industry, on what healthcare is and where it's going. So, first, why don't we call on ROCKY TARANTELLO.

Dr. R. Tarantello, CRE
Tarantello & Associates
Newport Beach, CA

TARANTELLO: Before I cover some of the issues I wanted to outline for you, I want to give you just a little bit of background in what brings us here. About 15 years ago an old college friend called me. I'd been in the real estate industry for about 25 or 30 years, doing real estate consulting and serving on the faculty of USC, so he figured I knew something about it. Neither of those credentials necessarily mean that I do, but he thought I did. He said, "I've just been hired as the CEO of a small medical practice." He went on to explain that "we have one clinic, one administrative office, approximately 15 to 20 physicians, and 8,000 enrollees in managed care plans." This was a time in which managed care was virtually unheard of. I began to exclusively represent that managed care physician group in facilities acquisitions about 15 years ago, and we ultimately ended up acquiring 15 clinical facilities, a 164-bed hospital, and, last year, a high identity major corporate headquarters for executive offices, record storage and supply distribution. We now enroll in excess of 100,000 patients under managed care contracts. And then, of course, along the way you discover a great deal about the healthcare business. I've learned a great deal from the physicians. I've learned a great deal from the people that were in the healthcare industry. I'm still primarily in real estate consulting by and large, but having acquired several hundred thousand square feet of space for my client serving virtually all of their various facilities' functions, from executive headquarters to clinical facilities to record storage, has heightened my awareness of the market impact of managed care.

This case is a classic example of how a primary care group used its real estate decision-making process in very strategic ways. Real estate isn't something, for this group at least, that is adjunct. It is a strategic tool of the new healthcare business, and that's how I intend to present it to you here. It is well-known by virtually all people who have even a casual connection with the healthcare industry that the demand for healthcare is rising and compensation per patient is falling. We all know that.

I began to focus on real estate as a strategic tool when I learned that facilities represent the second greatest cost of the groups that I have come in contact with, after personnel. And while there are frequent evaluations of personnel efficiency, I have yet to see a healthcare group that does much to evaluate the efficiency of their facilities. I've made many presentations to other healthcare organizations and asked them how they evaluate the efficiency of their facilities. How many square feet per physician, how many square feet per nurse station, what are your patient loads, what are your required parking ratios? I've found it nearly impossible to find any standards of practice. The only standards I have been able to use are the individual standards that we set on a client-by-client basis. The industry has failed miserably by not establishing criteria to evaluate the efficiency of their facilities. There is virtually no consistency among managed care groups regarding patient per square foot ratios, physicians per square foot ratios or non-physician employees per square foot relationships.

Moreover, the healthcare facility is much more than simply a place to do business. In particular, we can employ locational strategy to preempt our competitors. When primary care providers negotiate contracts with insurance carriers, you must have a sufficient number of patient service locations on the map. Consequently, we use our clinical locations as a strategic preemption device. We also use our facilities as a marketing tool. We choose locations offering great visibility to our facilities. We choose to locate at specific sites which offer a very highly visible location and ease of access. This fosters patient satisfaction and good public relations. We have also found that newly constructed facilities achieve greater patient utilization sooner than some of the retrofitted or older leased facilities. And then, lastly, there is a concept in business which we can refer to as franchise value.

Certain locations are superior to others and in the long run develop a value beyond the singular value of the real estate. This franchise or network value provides an opportunity to capitalize on such details as locational convenience, access and adequate parking.

The availability of other related retail services as well as building design and signage can also play a part. This is just a quick summary on how we go about doing our general planning for facilities.

Depending on the patient load expected in a particular facility, we configure our clinical facilities into 4,000 square foot increments. A very small facility would range from 12,000 to 16,000 square feet. Larger facilities, depending on patient load, may end up at 30,000 square feet. Ultimately, it is the geographic dispersion of the facilities that allows the group to effectively penetrate the regional healthcare market and claim greater value for the whole than the sum of the individual parts.

Controlling the costs of new acquired facilities is difficult at best. We may take advantage of real estate market swings from a pure market cycle perspective, but there is little we can do about two very important issues--the enormous cost of new tenant improvements and the additional cost of additional parking requirements created by increased patient traffic.

As a consequence, it is very difficult to find facilities that will even begin to accommodate our patient loads and staffing requirements. The parking ratios of a typical office facility are approximately one parking space per 250 square feet, or one car per 250. With a typical 10,000 square foot building, we typically find a 40-space requirement, depending upon local jurisdiction. Due to the increased patient loads, physician counts and other staff at those facilities, we have found that a 6-to-1 ratio is the minimum requirement we will accept. At some facilities, we enjoy a ratio of 10-to-1. Even at higher ratios, we frequently fill the lot.

I'm used to negotiating facility leases, and assuming acquisitions, where we have a lot more latitude in what it costs for a new facility. What I've learned about healthcare facilities, is that we don't have a lot of latitude regarding cost. We can take advantage of ups and downs in the real estate market from a pure market cycle perspective. However, there isn't much we can do about two very important issues: the enormous cost of installing the facility, by virtue of the fact that we're generating more traffic per facility than traditional facilities ever generated.

As a consequence, we find it very difficult to find facilities that will even begin to accommodate our patient loads and our staff. Therefore, what I'm going to do very quickly for you here is to go over some details, rather than skimming over some of the other general provisions in the couple of minutes I have left. I'll give you a little bit of an idea of how this worked on a recent transaction. The parking ratios on a typical office facility are approximately one parking space for 250 square feet. One person per 250, which means that on a typical 10,000 square foot building, we have about a 40-space requirement, depending on the jurisdiction. Due to the increased patient loads, physician counts, and other staff at those facilities, we have found that six to one is the minimum requirement we will accept. I have some facilities that we park ten to one; ten parking spaces per 1,000 square feet of facility, and we fill it.

At certain times we experience spillover parking into the street. This is essentially a peak hour problem, which occurs at certain times of the day or on weekends. In any event, providing facilities with atypically high parking ratios causes higher facilities costs as additional land areas are utilized causing overall facilities costs to rise. This higher costs is compounded by the effect of substantially higher tenant improvement costs, or the cost of installing the interiors.

A typical office building interior build-out costs between $25 and $35 per square foot. However, we have found that when building from scratch, bare shell and core, we can usually do it for about $50 to $55 per square foot. Surprisingly, when retrofitting, it usually costs between $65 and $75 per square foot. In many cases, it's actually cheaper to tear the building down and start from the foundation up than it is to try to retrofit an existing facility.

You might ask, why pay these higher costs? If that facility happens to occupy a strategic location, from a market penetration standpoint, that's a location we must have. It doesn't matter if a few extra dollars must be spent on the interior of the building. We are driven by location strategy.

Daniel M. Cain
Cain Brothers & Company, Incorporated
New York, NY

CAIN: Welcome to the world of contradictions. For those who are not in the healthcare industry, it's going to be a little bit like Alice's walk through Wonderland; trying to understand the contradictions that affect real estate and healthcare delivery, and the strains that society has put on providers. Cost, access, quality. I think it's interesting, you should read the medical journals and read the front page of the business section, and how there are contradictions between perceptions that the value of hospitals is decreasing when on the other hand, there is a tremendous amount of acquisitions of hospitals.

On the other hand, every time a hospital goes up for sale, there is a big war to acquire it.

It's interesting that the darling of Wall Street right now with respect to healthcare happens to be a hospital company called BBCA. There's leasing down, and buying of assets that the rest of the world seems to think is in excess. Today, we'll go through and analyze the opportunities and risks, with respect to healthcare and real estate. It might be interesting to try to frame the principle forces that are reshaping this industry. There is a transition from fee for service medicine to capitated medicine, where the buyers are given a budget in advance to take care of the fixed numbers of hundreds of thousands of patients. It's up to their creativity and ingenuity, to be able to provide that care within those financial constraints.

That will tremendously change the financial incentives of providers to be efficient or bear the risk of that transition. Secondly, these cost pressures are going to force more and more aggregation of ownership, ranging from endangered pharmaceutical companies to the neighboring physician practice.

You've got to be bigger to obtain the leverage, and the economies of scale percentages, in order to compete in a reimbursement environment. It's interesting, a very creative client, Sunnyvale Health System, which is located in Southern California, has gone on record as saying that under managed care, a hospital may mean a recognition of failure in providing good quality health maintenance. Their definition of quality healthcare is somebody who is in their system that ends up living 15% to 20% longer than their life expectancy, who ends up never being admitted to a hospital, and finally dies at home in their bed, at age 80 to 85, after just having experienced wonderful sex. If that's the product they're selling, I think there are a lot of people out there who want to buy it.

The third thing that's changing healthcare is the ability to differentiate quality. It used to be you'd go around the country (Sherwin and I have certainly done this), to every hospital whether it was a Catholic hospital, a Jewish hospital, a community hospital, or a public hospital, all saying, "we stand for quality." Nobody could define what that quality meant. Now, firms like SHERWIN's information and technology systems are available, and the provider is going to able to obviously differentiate why you should use one system of managed healthcare versus another.

Thereafter, as consumers, we have to be able to make more informed decisions, which will separate those who are in the business, with those who are leaders in business. Thirdly, in order to provide services, and be competitive in this industry, you're going to see a rapid consolidation. Whether it's a hospital, the physicians in a surgery center, or the surgery center and a hospice, we have an industry that grew up with all these different color reimbursement dollars. We have red dollars for hospitals, green dollars that go to physicians, and blue dollars that go to outpatient surgery. Now, under capitation, we just have a single dollar that everybody is trying to seize. You're going to see bigger boulders in the healthcare delivery system, and as you see these bigger boulders, whether they're physician group practices, HMOs, or hospitals, you are also going to see great opportunities for innovative start-up companies. These innovative start-up companies are looking for a specific niche in order to have a competitive edge.

Lastly, looking at opportunities in the healthcare sector, you have to be aware that there's a fundamental, philosophical and political shift taking place not only in Washington, but around the country; and that is that competition is the way we're going to control healthcare costs and improve its quality. The implications of that with respect to a major portion of this industry, and the not-for-profit hospitals, are no longer the justification for giving away free care and community services, more than they're receiving in terms of exemptions from property taxes, income taxes, and bonds. Maybe the Republican philosophy is that not-for-profit forms of ownership, whether it's the HMO, the hospital or medical groups, may be an impediment to this competition. I think you're going to see more boards of directors of hospitals, more and more legislators, and more and more people in Washington who are saying we need containment of costs through more competition.

If not-for-profit forms of ownership impede competition, then maybe we need to address a more level playing field. I think, in that transition, starting in boards as well as state legislatures is necessary in order to establish a reconfiguration of the ownership structure. In my opinion, this competition, these forces, whether they're technology, costs, or an aggregation, are going to create some tremendous opportunities for innovative ways of packaging the housing of healthcare services and deliveries. Fortunately, now healthcare has gone from about 11% to 12% of the gross national product in the seventies, to 14% of the gross national product. It's going to continue to grow to 15% or 16%, in spite of all these cost containment goals, because of the demographics in this country, the lifestyle of the American people, and because of their insistence on quality and access. More importantly, we feel that 16%, 17% or 18% of the gross national product may be the best place for the use of resources. What better service to offer than healthcare and mental care? I'm not sure that the constraints are going to be on whether we're spending too much money, but whether we're getting quality and output with respect to those dollars.

Secondly, with this market differentiation, those who are efficient managers of resources are going to get more opportunities, which will be taken away from those independent providers who can no longer make this transition. It's interesting. When I came into the securities industry, it was at the time we went from fixed commissions on Wall Street to negotiated commissions. Every business school in America has these wonderful tombstones that were put together to sell stocks or bonds in General Motors or Caterpillar Tractor. Moreover, they cancel these firms that no longer exist, because they weren't able to make the transition to what society needed, as we went through this process of industry de-regulation.

Lastly, the real estate aspects of healthcare delivery have gone from everything being in giant hospitals, to a decade where we tried to diversify by taking those services out of the hospital, and putting them in office buildings, surgery centers, different forms of cheaper delivery; simply because of the reimbursement flow of dollars.

In the 1990's, I think we're going to see this aggregation process take place once again, where the services come back to a central location. Then you end up with these large hospitals that are no longer used to store sick patients, but will provide all the other services that are needed to maintain wellness in an insured group. Whether that wellness is provided over the telephone, the fax machine, through an educational form, or through an intensive care unit, you're going to have this huge reconfiguration of the marketplace. The hospital will continue to be the Mecca of where healthcare is provided. People will come to a single location, as opposed to the philosophy, and the theory of the 1980's, where it was cheaper to take those services and fragment them across cheaper forms of providers. With respect to the opportunities here, I think that the ownership of healthcare real estate is going through a major transformation.

Certainly with respect to the investor-owned, they will realize a substantial difference between managing, having control over assets, and having title to assets. If you look at the not-for-profits, which still control the bulk of healthcare resources in the country, they need to have this percentage of their overall assets allocated to bricks and mortar. It's the expectation that the value of these assets is going to continue to increase, and there's a danger to holding title. It would make more sense to have another sophisticated investor deal with them, which is so much more common when you step outside healthcare, and look at other capital intensive industries. The Sheraton Hotel, for instance, is not owned by the bricks and mortar of this hotel.

Today, I think opportunities are emerging for both the investor and people who are innovative in transitioning. This used to be defined as a hospital. It will be interesting to see how the next generation of health care users and managers of health care will look at our situation today, look back at the Nehru suits, and the cars with the big, giant fins, and ask how can you think this applies to us? It doesn't. There is going to be a bit of chaos, and in its place will be a much more efficient, user-friendly form of receiving health care.

Michael D. Stephens
President & CEO
Hoag Memorial Hospital Presbyterian
Newport Beach, CA

STEPHENS: Let's see if I can beat nine minutes. We've had a discussion on real estate and finance. The objective of my presentation is to determine how we deal with these issues in order to operate our health facilities more cost effectively. I'm going to talk about some paradigms and perspectives on conventional wisdom, and then give you my perspective on some of the strategies that have been utilized by those of us who operate health facilities and systems and the change taking place around us.

First of all, the paradigms: One of the few things that I know about facility design and real estate is something I learned a long time ago, and that is that form follows function. The problem that I have is I can't identify the function in this rapidly changing health care environment. Because of that I'm not quite certain what forms our new facilities and real estate holdings are going to take. But that is certainly the challenge facing us and why seminars such as this one are so important.

Our industry used to be quite predictable. Things have changed dramatically. It reminds me of someone who observed that everyone knows what a unicorn looks like, but no one has ever seen one. This applies to so many of the concepts we currently embrace. Everybody talks about them as if they are commonly understood, but no one's ever actually seen one at work in its pure form.

My second observation: If you've seen one solution or model, you've seen one solution or model. It is very difficult--and increasingly more so--to transport one strategy to another facility or operation. There are several dynamics involved now that you really are developing solutions to situations that are unique, and you can't apply what works from one situation to another to the extent we used to. Think back to the `70s health planning review when health planning was still part of the scene in this state. Hospitals were often accused of having an edifice complex. And I think to an extent that was true. Our sense of achievement, our sense of worth, our fundamental values; were reflected in how large and how imposing our physical structures had become. Now compare that edifice complex with what, I think, we're facing now. The transition--or a revolution if you will--to something along the lines of not horizontal or vertical integration, but virtual integration. We are talking now in the context of how can we avoid a financial downfall because of our ownership of large capital assets.

First, how can we use our assets more effectively? How can we end this dependence on asset ownership? How can we accomplish this by not having our assets tied conventionally in real estate? The challenge facing someone who's involved in health care and has been through this transition--and happens to be very heavily involved with facilities and structures--is what do I do with these facilities that are increasingly under-utilized? Secondly, how can I anticipate the future of health care delivery and how am I going to develop strategies which will be responsive? And thirdly, how do I deploy my assets to pursue the kinds of strategies that are necessary in order to be competitive?

Two outlined strategic responses have been utilized to date in transforming our organizations. The first is traditional downsizing, or as more popularly called--rightsizing, work redesign, benchmarking, or re-engineering. The consequences are clearly excess capacity and unutilized facilities. We are currently in the process of trying to convert this excess capacity to more productive uses, and as a result debt really becomes an issue of financial survival. If you have debt, it's like an albatross around your neck, because that debt is represented -- by and large -- by facilities that aren't as economically utilized as they have been in the past.

I think the prognosis for this strategy--which is basically to either sell and get out of the business or downsize and circle the wagons in an attempt to become a more efficient entity -- might be effective in an undifferentiated market, where the basic product is undergoing very little technological and structural change. That certainly doesn't describe health care, and so by definition I don't think that downsizing is a long-term strategy, or even an intermediate one. I think it's a short-term survival strategy while the industry sorts itself out. Health care is changing dramatically, both in terms of structural changes in relationships and technology. You cannot just stand on the side, you will not survive the long run.

That takes us to the next strategy, which is more prevalent now. We're probably seeing much more of it in the last year or two. This is the strategy that relies on increasing the size of the health care organization to provide the necessary economies of scale that allow you to be more effective in maintaining your current lines of business. The concept is as follows: (1) You get more leverage and a better price because you are a larger entity and can negotiate better terms from the insurance carriers, or health plans, suppliers, or even physicians; (2) you have a geographic coverage in these consolidated organizations that allows you to position yourself more effectively to contract as consolidated providers as health plans and insurance companies merge. Every merger begets a corresponding merger on the other side; and (3) you merge so you can more effectively utilize your resources. This has the most promise, but is the most difficult to achieve because the fundamental mission and historical role of merged entities is changed.

As an example, rather than three hospitals performing open-heart surgery, the maximum operating efficiency is achieved at 1,000 operations a year. If those three hospitals are each doing 300, then the real tough choices are clear.

First, which hospital will do the 1,000 procedures; and second, what happens to the other two organizations with respect to the excess capacity created with the consolidation? These decisions are always the last to occur in the conversion process because there are inevitably winners and losers.

The tactic is merger and alliances. The results, I think, create some of the same issues, but on a larger scale. The focus is still on physical assets. It perpetuates the idea that horizontal and vertical integration of capacity assets is going to be a viable strategy in the long term. I believe it is an intermediate strategy at best. It does not address the central issue, which is, how can at best. It does not address the central issue, which is, how can assets be employed and deployed more effectively? What, increasingly, we should be looking at and talking about where success is not defined by asset accumulation, the focus is neither horizontal nor vertical integration of the physical assets but keeping your assets as liquid as possible so that you can apply them to the kind of integration strategies that are going to be necessary. Let somebody else own the assets.

As we develop creative ideas of how to use assets, the pride of ownership--this edifice complex if you will--will disappear among those of us who operate health care facilities. So that's the perspective: downsizing, consolidation, mergers--they've all been a part of the response to the changes occurring in our industry, but I think there's much more to be done. We should start looking at new concepts and configurations. The virtual organization places an emphasis not on physical assets or size, but will redefine the future role real estate investors and financial organizations will play in health care. Thank you.

Michael J. Calhoun
Lewis-VHI, Inc.
Sausalito, CA

CALHOUN: The health care industry is in foreclosure, and real estate is particularly vulnerable. The references heard this morning are not meant to deprecate anyone; the reference is real--about the common indicators. There are declining ratios between in-patient accommodations, and treatment and turnover. There are also declining concentrations going on in the field hospital, and these are real trends which are here to stay. Other trends that are more esoteric are indicators of fundamental change taking place in the industry, much like what happened in the steel industry in the '70s and '80s.

These developments are here to stay, but they suggest the dramatic changes not only required within the industry, but also in health thinking, and in the real estate industry. The discussion this morning suggests something that I found interesting here, and it is true. One of our first speakers said that this discussion is fraught with contradictions, and it is in the contradictions that I think enlightenment takes place. Passive hysteria takes place behind the headlines of the decline of the industry and the closing of hospitals. Of course, the information is very relevant. I'd like to capsulize it, in shorthand fashion, and in five observations of micro-issues behind the headlines.

First, the demand for health care services actually continues to exceed the rate of inflation and exceeds the rate of growth of population. If you look at the health plans, for example, which have very aggressive efforts to control health care expenditures, the expectation is for full implementation of the growth rate in health care.

Secondly, the quality and intensity of in-patient services that is being delivered today, largely in hospitals, is increasing even though the average census measures are in decline. Let me go through that again, because the implication of that is very significant. While the bed count is down, the intensity and quality of care being given in hospitals is actually increasing.

Thirdly, the volume and intensity of ambulatory care is increasing dramatically, and it is increasing in rough proportions to the decline of bed utilization in hospitals. The ratio and the multiplier are not quite clear right now. It's in the early stages, but there is a ratio relationship.

Fourthly, national statistics can be misleading about what's happening in the healthcare industry. It is a kind of comment that is reducing all events to a common observation. However, there are significant local verifications in both the variety and in the content of the rationalization which is taking place within the healthcare industry. It is in the local micro developments that the kinds of service are uppermost in your mind and need to be understood.

But finally, survival. Survival does not necessarily mean escaping this rationalization; you are nearly the same as you were when you went in. Survival probably means coming out differently. The tests ought to be that you came out, and not how you came out. What I would like to do is take those observations and test them against the market in the Los Angeles area.

Clearly, the influence of rising managed care contracts of HMOs and other kind of measures can have significant impact on the demand for beds. The managed care enrollment levels in Los Angeles County in 1990 were, for Medi-Cal approximately 40%, Medicare about 25%, and commercial insurers about 45%. Currently, those rates are increasing. Most importantly, by the year 2000, we estimate that managed care enrollment levels of Los Angeles County, for Medi-Cal, for example, will be about 70%. For Medi-Care, it's estimated to be about 45%, and for commercial providers, between 65% and 80%. The consequence of increased managed care and other kinds of consolidations taking place in the marketplace has tremendous impact on the days-per-thousand population.

In 1990, for example, the days-per-thousand population under managed care was about 500 for Medi-Cal. We're projecting that by the year 2000, it will be between 380 and perhaps 300. In commercial coverage, for example, in 1990, it was 350 days of the 1,000 population. We're projecting somewhere in the neighborhood of 180 to 120. Very dramatic figures! Medicare in 1990 was roughly 1,600, and we're looking at perhaps 800 to 700 by the year 2,000. This is roughly on the scale of 30, ranging from 30% to 60% decline on the days-per-1,000.

The contrast between the change for fee-for-service is roughly in the 20% to 35% range in reduction over this time period. What does that mean? Managed care rising incidents of contracts declined in days-per-1,000. On average, it appears from our estimates that Los Angeles County will have about a 40% to 50% reduction for beds by the year 2,000. Yet, at the same time there is this decline in demand for beds. There are a number of developments taking place. In the same time period, hospitals will result in an additional 27% decline in beds due to merged facilities and the need for modernization. Yet at the same time, the plans currently on the books for new facilities and new growth represent approximately an increase of 14%, incurred between now and the year 2,000. Therefore, in factoring out the facilities decline and demand for hospital beds, there is almost an offset of 2/3 of the decline that will be made up by increased billing in facilities.

In violative aspects, there is a tremendous contradiction that you can expect coming out of what actually is taking place in the marketplace. In Los Angeles County, the expectation currently is that the demand for maternity care and delivery service by the year 2,000, will be under demand. One of the most dramatic areas where there is current undercapacity is in emergency room services. That's our thumbnail sketch of the kinds of things that are happening in this County. Across the country, the kinds of niche[?] changes that are taking place are rather significant. Those are some general guidelines about what is happening in healthcare.

The first and most significant factor is that there is not a decline throughout health care; what is taking place is an increase in the demand for healthcare outside the hospital. There are geographical differentiations that are also significant. Ambulatory care facilities are developed by physician networks. There is new demand for inpatient facilities, even in hospitals.

While the facilities will be smaller, they will be more intensive because the new concepts in care delivery require the facilities. Therefore, even existing facilities that are functioning well now will not be able to continue.

Finally, there are those in partnerships, with a rise in health services and others who are dependent upon health services, such as the real estate agent. Survival most likely means a fundamental adjustment in the business approach from the quantitative approach; building large buildings that are for fixed use, to a more qualitative approach, and looking at facilities that provide high technology and highly sophisticated services. There are services that are more user friendly. Those are more available. The theme for the 90's to be maintained is quality not quantity, where intensity is not spared.

IMPLEMENTING THE HEALTH CARE FACILITIES AUDIT

The Health Care Facilities Audit "Matrix"

IMPLEMENTING THE HEALTH CARE FACILITIES AUDIT

The Health Care Facilities Audit "Matrix"

In this Part II, we examine:

- **Taking Inventory--Assets and Liabilities.** What are our "hard assets"? Land. Buildings. Equipment. What is the condition of these assets? What is the debt structure and related cash flow demand associated with these assets? How has occupancy and usage changed in the past few years? How is it likely to change over the next few years?

- **Evaluating the Alternatives--Identifying the Problems and the Solutions.** What business(es) are we in? What related problems are we experiencing and how do these problems impact cash flow and/or occupancy and usage of our hard assets? What business(es) are we likely to be in the coming year? What related problems are we likely to experience and how will these problems impact cash flow and/or occupancy and usage of our hard assets? Will current hard assets be of any use in our likely future business(es)? Will change(s) in these hard assets be required? Will these changes be permitted by applicable regulations? Will cash flow from our likely future business(es) be sufficient to meet existing debt? If not, what capital formation alternatives are available to reduce existing debt?

- **"Costing" The Solutions--Using Industry "Protocols," "Matrices" and "Benchmarks" to Project Revenues and Expenses.** What are the industry "protocols" and "matrices" used to project future revenues and expenses? What are the related "benchmarks"? How have we compared to date? How are we likely to compare based upon assumed changes? How do projected revenues and expenses compare to past revenues and expenses? What iterations produce what changes? Consideration of applicable accounting principles.

Sherwin L. Memel, Esquire
Manatt, Phelps & Phillips
Los Angeles, CA

MEMEL: There is a need for implementing healthcare facilities. You heard earlier speakers talk about benchmarks and guidelines. One of the things we believe is necessary in order to develop a bank of information, comes and goes, and is really missing in this industry; hopefully we're going to receive some of this information from Ron Barak.

Ronald S. Barak, Esquire
Manatt, Phelps & Phillips
Los Angeles, CA

BARAK: Having heard some of the more general introductory remarks, we're now going to see if we can rise to the challenge of becoming a little more specific, something not that easy to do. On the one hand, we have to take the blinders off and really bear down. On the other hand, we also have to make sure we don't get caught up in the old "paralysis by analysis." Among the alternatives, there are facilities that can be closed, and should be closed. There are multiple users of multiple facilities that maybe ought to join together in a smaller number of facilities. There are facilities being used for one purpose today that maybe ought to be examined for alternative uses. In order to make sure we leave some time after these individual panel presentations for a bit of a roundtable discussion, and to involve the audience in some questions and some give and take, I'm going to keep my introductions more brief and less eloquent than Sherwin did, but I do remind you that the resumes of all of our speakers are in the written materials that you each have.

We're going to have 5-1/2 speakers in this next group: Michael Bobrow is the design principal and founder of Bobrow, Thomas & Associates, here in their Los Angeles Office; Judy Ellison is the President of Quadrant Group, a healthcare planning organization also located in Los Angeles; Charles Harrison is an audit partner at Arthur Andersen and heads their Southern California healthcare practice; Marc Margulis is the managing director of Houlihan, Lokey, Howard & Zukin, a well known valuation firm; and the half person I referred to, Tony Roesch, a partner of Michael Bobrow, will join us for the roundtable question and answer session. Since you don't have a resume on Tony in the written materials, I will tell you that he is in their Chicago office; he is their planning principal and director of that Chicago office; and he recently directed the planning of a $600 million replacement facility for the Cook County Hospital in

Chicago. So Tony has been through a lot of the nuts and bolts issues that you may be feeling. These are our second panel speakers.

Michael Bobrow, AIA
Bobrow/Thomas and Associates (BTA, Inc.)
Los Angeles, CA

MICHAEL BOBROW'S "IMPLEMENTING THE HEALTHCARE FACILITIES AUDIT"

(Mr. Bobrow's comments were unable to be transcribed)

Judy Pierson Ellison
Quadrant Group, Inc.
Los Angeles, CA

THE STRATEGIC REALITIES OF HOSPITAL REAL ESTATE LIABILITIES

Presented by Judy Pierson Ellison, MSN
President, Quadrant Group, Inc.

ELLISON: **Introduction.** Real estate -- the darling of hospital executives in the past decade -- has become a potential liability nightmare that administrators hope to avoid. But forward thinking organizations are pursuing strategies that will align their real estate with the market and reduce the burden of underutilized space to support the bottom line and preclude the risk of foreclosures.

Hospitals have not traditionally viewed themselves in the real estate business and yet, have expanded their real estate holdings and magnificent edifices over the last few decades. Empires have certainly been built, not intentionally as a line of business, but as "resources." Consequently, these often massive holdings have not been expertly managed and now have become real liabilities.

The Problem. The problem is that hospitals are now in the wrong business, carrying heavy debts on overbuilt, single-use buildings. The fact is that more medical care is being given outside of what are perceived by medical groups and health plans as "those expensive" hospitals. Physicians now know how, and are financially incentivized, to put fewer patients in the hospital for shorter periods of time, if they admit them at all. To today's medical care groups who are the brokers for patients, hospitals are cost centers -- liabilities to their risk pools, and to be avoided.

In fact, there are too many hospitals and too many hospital beds for the utilization that can be expected with new trends in treatment and managed care. Milliman and Robertson has released figures that show that in a well managed HMO, the days per 1000 enrollees will go from 450 to 172 annually. Lengths of stay will be closer to 3 days instead of 5. There will simply not be enough patients to go around no matter how creative the marketing and niche program development is. The bottom line is that many hospitals will be closed, and the beds in those that survive will be converted to alternate uses.

Strategy 1 - Get Out of the Business. Hospitals need to consider getting out of the "hospital" business in order to survive with the real estate they have. Most will continue to maintain a few inpatient, short-stay surgical, obstetrics, geriatrically-oriented medical services and selected specialty programs -- only enough patients to fill probably half of their beds. Hospitals will need to take a hard-line approach and eliminate low volume or unprofitable inpatient services within the strategy of Product Line Accountability.

To make matters worse, the expensive traditional diagnostic services will need to be downsized. Most hospitals have found it almost impossible to keep the business when freestanding diagnostic centers or groups themselves offer more cost effective, consumer friendly services. Instead, hospitals need to consider outplacing expertise or telemedicine connections to group sites or nursing homes, none of which will need the hospital diagnostic spaces they now have. Within a regionally integrated network, diagnostic services will be closed that are duplicative with patients sent to "sister" facilities as a strategy to centralize and share highly specialized technological services.

Even Emergency services will be downsized while non-space-dependent services are developed to support telephone triage and extended group site office coverage. Groups will become much more effective in directing enrollees to alternatives such that only true emergencies, now estimated at 20% of an emergency department's volume, will show up in the hospital ER.

The proverbial "good news, bad news" is that there will be increased demand for Home Health, Skilled Nursing Facilities and Rehabilitative Sub-acute. The good news is that medical/surgical units can be converted to these uses. The bad news is that it will be expensive to convert, for example, to a SNF, and the reimbursement will not be as high as acute care despite an initial cost-based reimbursement period in which capital costs are included in the payment.

Hospitals with true foresight anticipate extending services out into the community, not on an isolated campus. This trend does not bode well for real estate and debt ridden hospital campuses.

The bottom line is that hospitals will be less a place than an interconnected system of health care services delivered beyond the walls of the real estate.

Strategy 2 - Reduce the Liability. The liabilities associated with the fixed, underutilized real estate must be reduced. All hospitals are aggressively restructuring operations and redesigning to break even under the current capital debt loads by:

- Consolidating patients into more efficient sized units to be able to close beds and cut operating costs or to reuse them for less acute functions
- Remodeling units for patient-focused care which enables more efficient use of space and point-of-service care delivery which reduces costs
- Redesigning outpatient services and spaces to become more efficient and customer friendly in an attempt to keep or regain the outpatient business controlled by the medical groups
- Creating healing environments that are home-like and family-centered to become more acceptable and responsive to patients to regain their loyalty
- Bringing off-site leased space that had been moved off campus back into unused hospital wings to eliminate rent of those spaces

While these changes require some capital themselves, the investment is often necessary to be able to cut the overhead. The spaces, as they are currently designed and used, add overhead that cannot be borne under today's payment schedules. Hospitals have to better utilize the space in order to better utilize the people, and attempt to garner the business they can from their market areas, even if it isn't by offering the high tech programs of years past.

Strategy 3 - Convert Liabilities to Assets. The real estate liabilities must be converted into assets. Hospitals need to provide primary care physician groups with space and administrative support. Unfortunately, this may mean building yet more buildings. Often the existing Medical Office Buildings may be strategic liabilities -- they may not accommodate medical group practices, but are often filled with specialists, not primary care physicians. Unless the specialists can be moved out, which is unlikely, new real estate may need to be leased or built. Certainly, this is a situation in which some expert real estate, long-range planning is needed.

The safest way to maintain utilization of the existing hospital services, albeit at lower volumes, is by investing capital into building an integrated physician network of primary care groups that will direct patients to the hospital. This investment usually means capital for managed care management systems and interlinked information systems --- not buildings; this concept is often a difficult one for non-profit Boards to understand since they know they can raise funds for a building, but for an information system?

It may be that hospitals will have to invest in these integrated networks with physicians in order to protect their credit ratings. Standard & Poors announced in early 1995 that hospitals with limited services and weak physician associations may find their credit ratings in jeopardy if they allow reform and managed care to pass them by.

Bottom Line - Use it or lose it! Hospitals must redesign their operations and facilities to provide more of a non-acute care focus and to cut the overhead of operations. The name of the game in old reimbursement models was volume -- get volume above the break-even operational point and make money. Under managed care with capitated, fixed or reduced payment, the game is to bring the overhead down below the anticipated annual allocation expected from the business. Thus, the burden of high operational costs in inefficient facilities and the burden of debt on underutilized spaces or buildings cannot be tolerated.

The first approach is certainly to try to contract for enough enrollment to provide a revenue stream to cover the ongoing overhead. However, without access to a large enrollment base, revenue will not cover overhead expenses, much less debt. The next approach then has to be to reduce the overhead -- to cut staff, to take underutilized space out of service, to get rid of unnecessary leases and, in some cases, to sell buildings for which there is no longer any justified use. If hospitals are to be competitive "cost centers" in managed care, they will have to become lean and mean machines.

Many hospitals will not be able to make these changes as solo hospitals, so the industry is experiencing a sale and merger mania. The real estate management issues are then, however, exacerbated as regional systems of affiliated or owned hospitals look at sharing of services, expertise and space in a more rational basis.

Many hospitals will be bought and then closed. What then will be their real estate value? Nursing homes? Jails? The problem is, of course, the limited use of highly specific and technical spaces. Some hospitals are finding it cheaper to raze the building and sell the land.

Conclusion. The transformation of hospitals must draw upon new solutions to manage patient care, manage hospital costs, manage health care delivery systems and manage capital investments and assets. Hospitals need to close the door on old solutions in order to maintain and support real estate that become competitive advantages, not liabilities.

In a Managed Care World, Volume Yields Loss . . .

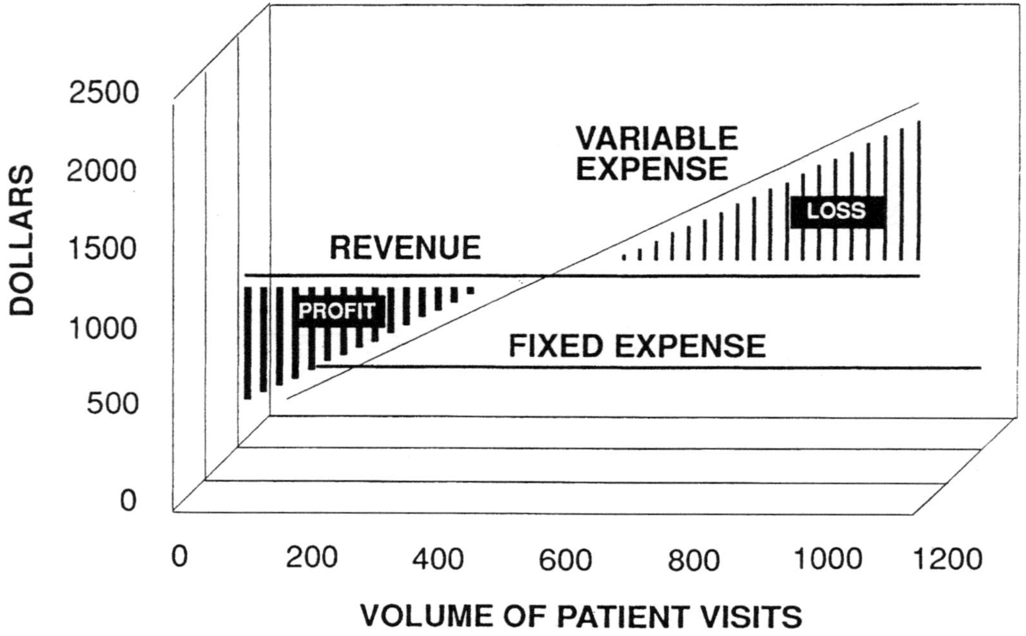

Source: Integrated Healthcare Report, May 1993

QUADRANT

HCIREI Speech/2-9-95

Seamless Continuum of Care

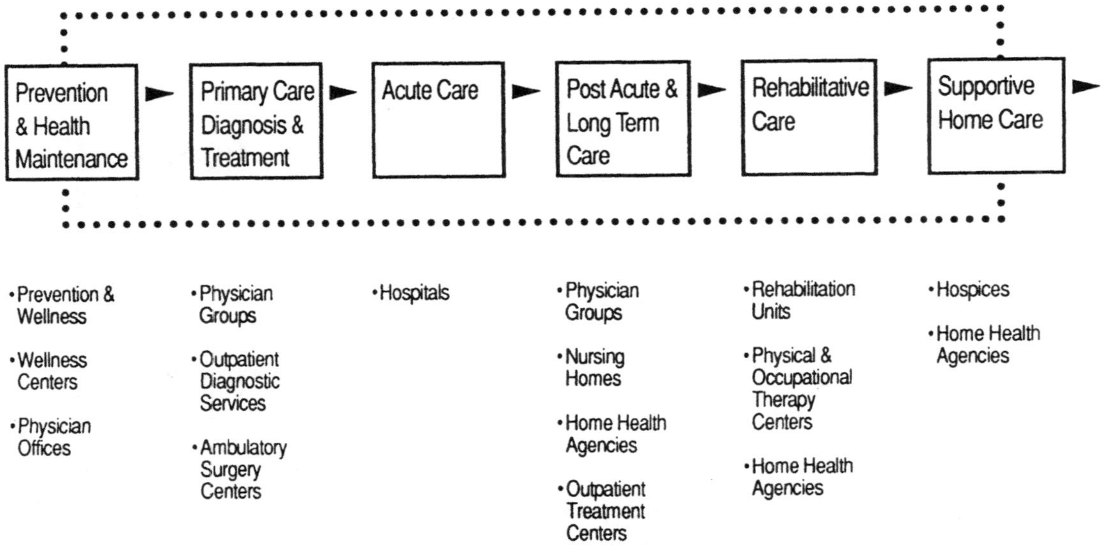

QUADRANT

Total Inpatient Utilization Rates in Managed Care System

	Loosely Managed	Moderately Managed	Well Managed
# of Admits Per 1000	83.70	70.80	57.42
ALOS	5.38	4.19	3.11
# of Days Per 1000	450	296	172

Source: Milliman and Robertson, 1994

QUADRANT

HCIREI Speech/2-9-95

Charles Harrison
Arthur Andersen & Co.
Los Angeles, CA

HARRISON: We've talked to you about the hot air balloon thing. We're in a balloon, a hot air balloon. You must be a CPA. Why would you say that? What I want to do is elaborate a little bit on what Judy talked about. I'd like to discuss some accounting issues and tax issues, and how tax issues create more accounting issues. Certainly, hospitals seem to be over-bedded and under utilized. This cartoon has a bunch of people standing outside the hospital. You don't see the room that they're running through because they don't pay for a room. That's the whole idea of same-day service. According to all my clients, probably the best utilization is maybe 75% at County Hospital, but I think that we're going to see a lot of hospitals that aren't doing too well. Some are going to want to change their services; some are going to want to get out of business; some will get out of business. If they do that, what are they going to change to? There are a couple of accounting things that we can talk about. We've talked about changing the use of assets; there's no simple silver bullet and no simple answers. There's one that looks pretty simple. That would be a possible write-down.

For example, you have a hospital, and you have hired some consultants, but your being a hospital just isn't going to be successful for you. You just can't make money because you have too much competition. You're in the wrong business. You really need to be a Pizza Hut. Pizza Hut would be a good business; we have 400 private dining rooms. However, what you have is a building that is probably over cost. Then the idea of a write-down would be to reduce the cost of that building, anticipate a sale, run it like a Pizza Hut or a skilled nursing facility. Well, why would you want to do that? You would want to do that because you have this terrific amount of depreciation, and while it's only 6%, it's still a huge number; and if you want to test or find out what the true operations are in the skilled nursing facility, or Pizza Hut or whatever you create, you're going to need to get the depreciation problem solved. Then there's an opportunity to do a write-down of that asset to take it down to where we need to. You will have some operating results relative to whatever you change the use to. The operation of the building will be effective, whatever you've chosen to be. That is all predicated on the supposition that your accountant has no mercy. You can estimate at least on the cost of the square footage that you will get where you want to be. It is a one-time hit. It's not pleasant, and it may not even get you to where you want to go. Why? Most of you who aren't in the hospital business will soon learn that all hospitals in Southern California that are not-for-profit probably have some form of tax problems.

For example, St. Johns in Santa Monica, and they have debt now. The trouble with tax-exempt debt is that it is the result of your tax-exempt status. Your facility may not meet the criteria the IRS had in mind when giving tax-exempt status. If you don't convert to something within the tax-exempt status, that debt could quickly be taxable. Many have the idea that they do not have to pay taxes if the business or facility becomes taxable. The next thing the IRS does is look at your tax-exempt status. You may pay higher taxes if you lose your tax-exempt status. You might have unrelated business income taxes depending on the kind of business to which this building and your operation convert. There are state and local taxes, property taxes, state taxes, city taxes, and lots of other taxes, not just taxes on the status of the business.

The biggest asset on a not-for-profit balance sheet is the tax-exempt status; it's on the ability to not pay taxes and the ability to do with tax-exempt debt. There are some real problems that strain what a building can be used for. For example, the number of beds can strain a hospital. Change the building too much or change it into a skilled nursing facility -- that's probably okay. However, the result is that you are over cost and probably oversized. Change the building to anything that's going to compete with the private sector, and you might lose your tax-exempt status.

Marc Margulis
Houlihan, Lokey, Howard & Zukin
Los Angeles, CA

MARGULIS: It's interesting how each of us approaches the issue of health care. From my perspective, the issue comes down to maximizing your profits in order to survive. The process of maximizing profits over value is operational. For-profit facilities increase profit facility for its shareholders. However, for not-for-profit, an increased profit facility benefits the organization. Therefore, I think the process that we have to consider, and the concept that I don't think many tend to think of, is reviewing our profit distribution. I'm surprised that the process of maximizing the value illustrated in this slide hasn't come up earlier in the presentations that we discussed today. You have to start with market analysis, operations review, loss accounting (which is supplied by accountability), organizational assessments, M/A opportunities, tax planning evaluation services, and access to capital. All this information benefits the management and advisors of the organization.

Strategies can be divided on the left side as a financial strategy and the right side as operational strategies. The results are new markets, new products, new systems, new structuring, and streamlining. Those strategies have to be analyzed in terms of the criteria that the organization has established or for their selection of the full-view approach. If it's all done right, everyone will wind up with more dollars.

The greatest dollar investment in the public market place is still in Med-Surg hospitals, followed by HMO's. This one here is a nursing site and these are critical care hospitals. This is physician group, home health, and special outpatient services. Now, even though this excludes the unprofitable publicly traded company, the private company for profit, and the wholly not-for-profit, this distribution does not seem long-term. Now, we then develop two hypotheses. The first was that the marketplace over the last few years with transition dollars has moved from asset investment to financial service related companies. In other words, the total market value of the companies that are heavily dependent on the dollar value of companies engaged in each network. We developed an index using just these criteria, and we found out that unfortunately the top lines here are HMO's and home health, followed by physician groups and outpatient specialty companies. Generally, what we see here is that over the last five years the total invested capital in these companies has increased substantially. Interestingly enough, you don't see a substantiation of the hypothesis when it comes to the assets of this company. The top line is long-term care, the second one is Med-Surg hospitals, and nursing is down at the bottom.

Now, of course, like I said, this data is biased. For one thing, the hospital section in this line over the last five years is for any industry in transition. The market in transition has an opportunity to take risks and hopefully gain support in order to ensure that companies are still escalating in value.

The second hypothesis is that we would see an inverse relationship between the asset intensiveness of the company and the multiple duration by which the market referenced the value of these companies. What we looked at were the multitudes of assets, revenues, and as a surrogate of asset intensiveness, use the asset turnover, which roughly is the amount of dollars that each dollar invested in the book value of the assets. Interestingly enough, what we see is that the turnover ratio for HMO's or suppliers in 1994 was 2.2 dollars of revenue for every dollar of asset invested, followed by physician groups and outpatient services, and home health down at the bottom. The asset-intensive group is at the top, long-term care is second, then nursing/convalescent, Med-Surg hospitals and such. The turnover ratio is consistent with direct costs.

And what we found, interestingly enough, to support the second hypothesis is that there is a very high degree of correlations between the asset turnover ratio's independent variable and the price of total assets and the price after total ratio. In other words, the greater the independence and total assets, the lower would be the ratios by which your market capitalizes.

Therefore, so what conclusions can be reached in 15 minutes on very astute and biased data? The conclusions are the obvious. That is that dollars should be extracted from health care facilities where possible, and investments in health care in the future should be limited where possible to maintenance and necessary replacements of facilities. Available invested dollars should go into substitute care, alternative care and physician networks.

MEMEL: I think we're seeing that what we will have continuing throughout the day is contradiction and difference of view on some of these subjects. Whether or not to invest in new or smaller facilities for more intensive uses, or whether to move into the substitute areas where long term care is somewhat adversary on the number two panels. Maybe they're not inconsistent; maybe there's a time and place for each strategy, depending on who you are. We will now further discuss with our panelists the subjects they raised. Does anyone have a first question in the audience?

QUESTION: I'd like to ask Mike Bobrow about the status of the earthquake standard in this whole equation. What is the impact of what happened in the earthquake on the health care issues in California?

BOBROW: That's a very good and a very important question for everybody who is involved with a hospital in California. The status report on the survivability of hospitals that were studied by the State showed that 75% of the space did not meet requirements of the post-1973 requirements. Since the Northridge earthquake, I think we are all very familiar with what's happened with older hospitals, even post-'73 buildings. Basically, we have not been able to find up until very recently a good solution. In California I believe the standards just came out making earlier standards more difficult. We are now requiring a substantial number of tests for every single connection within any proposed building. The building code is now nationwide. We're going to start to see these standards in Missouri, the Carolinas, New York and upper parts of the mid-west. The seismic problems that we have seen here are going to be a national type of problem. What does that do to an institution where a percentage of its facilities is pre-'73? Post-'73 buildings may not even meet those standards.

MEMEL: Ron, you have a question.

BARAK: What are you experiencing and what are your clients experiencing in terms of the various changing forces to which we've heard some reference and with which you must interact, whether it's land use regulators that you have to convince to permit you to make nonconforming changes in use, IRS staff that you have to convince not to upset tax exemptions when you make changes in uses originally approved for tax benefits, or private sector debt managers that aren't sure they have the authority to waive all restrictions in debt instruments?

STEPHENS: We're developing an ambulatory care campus on the property below our existing hospital site. It's 25 acres along which the highway sits below the bluff on which the hospital is located. Ironically, we will, hopefully, about this time be getting a vote from the Coastal Commission which will represent the end of a 4-1/2 year process going through local city approval entitlement massive plans through the Cultural/Coastal Commission hearings through a suit from Environmental Coalition once we receive Coastal Commission approval, which delays the final document findings by six months.

MEMEL: Thank you Mike. Is Al Smith here? Although he hasn't made his presentation yet, please give us some insight into how lenders look at some of these movements that have taken place, and Dan may be able to do so as well, where it requires relief from covenants or exceptions to be made . . . I know I've represented a couple of people where we've had to come to the lender to inform them and ask, for example, CitiBank: "Can we do this, please?"

SMITH: I think lenders generally are, if it makes business sense, going to understand what changes are necessary.

MEMEL: Do you think that the lenders are more familiar now than they might have been many years back in terms of what changes are taking place in the industry?

SMITH: As I'm going to say later, almost every major bank and regional bank now has its specific healthcare group. And many of those people have been involved in healthcare lending for maybe five years, so they understand the issues much more clearly today than earlier.

MEMEL: Thank you. Dan, did you want to make any comment?

CAIN: Banks and insurance companies and mutual funds are becoming less and less important. Where the power is now is the credit enhancers. Most people just don't want to buy a bond and assume that thirty-year risk. They want to be able to buy an MBIA or some type of guarantee.

BARAK: Speaking of bond-holders, this is one of the areas in which I think we are still trying to catch up. What often happens, when you decide you need a change in use from what the covenants in the bond issue permit, is that you find there isn't anyone set up to give this permission. You go to trustee who is in charge of the bond issue, who is guarding the bond holder's interests, and what he tells you is, under the bond instruments, he doesn't have any authority to do anything until there's a default. And you're not in default yet. What you're doing is being responsible and trying to address matters before you default. The answer you see is: "Well, you'll have to wait until you get into a little more trouble." If there's anything I've learned in the workout environment of the past few years, its that time is either your best friend or your worst enemy. When revenue has fallen below expenses, you have to stop the bleeding, and you have to do it quickly. I think there's an educational process that must take place here in terms of other healthcare seminars that you attend and at meetings and events where you have the opportunity to talk with the credit enhancers, land use regulators and tax authorities and get them to start focusing on these kinds of issues.

MEMEL: Perhaps we have just another minute or two before lunch. Tony, you had a very interesting experience in Oklahoma. Do you want to just give us a couple of minutes on that?

ROESCH: I think it's something that's relevant . . . the process that they've gone through and certainly the issues and trends that have been presented a handful of hospitals. We've done a fairly good analysis on the break-even point and where it's effective and not cost effective. From that, we've looked at what strategy can be developed and how to spend those dollars. It's very interesting that the focus has been to limit the dollars and the bricks and mortar, and really try to look at budgets and expenditures and things like technology and communications, and other types of things that really aren't factored in. Start to look at the professional planning and really look at the smaller facilities being designed for maximum use and flexibility within that environment.

MEMEL: Jerry Brown was right, smaller is better.

BOBROW: The other half of the question has to do with response to changes, has to do with what those changes might be for. One must look through alternative uses that are compatible to the community. Hospitals have been notoriously bad neighbors. I don't know of a hospital that is considered a good neighbor. The fear of hospitals as they stand right now will be a tremendous amount of traffic and 24 hour operation. If you look at the local changes where the opportunities are increased in the elderly area, we've found success in reusing portions of hospital communities, and we're very happy with that. You may have a business plan that could be used for a facility. But, because the hospital is operated under conditional use permits, they need permission for any change. They very thoroughly start working with that community and the acceptability of that alternative is extremely important for the success of the change.

MEMEL: We'll close for lunch. Our speaker will be SANDRA SMOLEY, the Secretary of Health and Welfare Agency or the State of California.

LUNCH PRESENTATION

MEMEL: I would like to introduce to you Sandra Smoley who is Secretary of the California Health and Welfare Agency. She was appointed as Secretary by Governor Pete Wilson in October 1993. She's a member of the Governor's cabinet, and she's an advisor on health and social service policy. She oversees two thousand employees and a total budget of $36 billion; she oversees twelve state departments and one board which are responsible for health. That's only one part of it. She also has oversight on social services and mental health, rehabilitation, developmental services, employment and a lot of other critical services to millions of people in California. She's been involved in the issues of statewide and national importance, including health reform. Before her present position, she was Secretary of the State's Consumer Services Agency. Sandy comes from a long history of experience in local government. In 1972 she was the first woman ever elected to the Board of Supervisors in Sacramento County and spent over 20 years on that Board, doing what she's doing now, balancing the growth of government on the one hand and the ever-growing demand for public services on the other. She has earned national recognition as the Presidential appointee to the major commission. She was President of California State Associations of Counties and National Association of Counties. She comes by our healthcare background naturally, since she was trained as a registered nurse at the University of Iowa. She's a graduate of the Senior Executive Training Program for State and Local Government at Harvard's John F. Kennedy School of Government. She has also done graduate work in economics at California State University in Sacramento. She's actively involved in a huge list of charitable volunteer endeavors and still manages to be a wife with two children. I'd like to introduce somebody I stand in awe of, Sandra Smoley.

Sandra R. Smoley, R.N.
Secretary
Health and Welfare Agency
State of California

SMOLEY: Thank you for having me here today. One of the things I get to do when the Governor can't do things is stand in for him. He is very sorry that he couldn't be with you today, but by the luck of the draw, you get me. But, that's alright too.

I was thinking about what I wanted to talk to you about today, so I called up Ed, and I said, "Gosh, Ed, what do you think I ought to talk about?" And he said, "Talk about regulations that will affect the health care industry." Then I called up Donald and said, "What do you think I ought to talk about?" And Don said, "Give us an overview of what the Governor has done with health care reform." But it was Sherwin who was the most succinct. He said, "Talk about ten minutes."

So I'm going to do all three, and then I'll leave time for you to ask me questions, and I'll try my best to answer them.

When Governor Wilson appointed me as his Secretary of Health and Welfare, I was excited and thrilled. As a registered nurse, I am really enjoying working on the important health issues that face our state.

But my responsibilities as Secretary go far beyond health care. I have 12 state departments, including the Employment Development Department, and one board reporting to me. The issues range from welfare reform to senior services to job training. I manage an agency which employs 42,000 and oversees a $36 billion budget.

A year ago after the Northridge earthquake I also had the responsibility of making sure all of you got what you needed to get your facilities up and running. I'd like to take a few minutes to talk about that.

One year ago you were at the center of the most damaging, costly earthquake in our nation's history. Governor Pete Wilson provided strong leadership in responding to this disaster, and the health care system was a top priority.

The Governor authorized starting interim non-structural repairs in numerous hospitals and health care facilities within hours of the quake to ensure that badly needed medical services would be available to victims.

One of my departments, the Office of Statewide Health Planning and Development (OSHPD), put damage survey teams into area hospitals and acute-care health facilities immediately after the quake, with the goal of putting them back into full operation as soon as possible.

Once the emergency needs were being met, we all turned our attention to clearing away the rubble. Governor Wilson, too, cleared away rubble by eliminating government-imposed obstacles and bureaucratic red tape so that rebuilding could begin immediately.

And once again, the health care system was a vital concern for Governor Wilson. Before the ground had stopped shaking, he personally directed me to come down to Los Angeles to cut the usual red tape and speed the reopening of damaged hospitals.

Hospital repair plans were given the highest priority for approval. Within days after the quake, I met with hundreds of hospital administrators, architects and engineers to help get their facilities back in business.

I was authorized to give on-site approvals for repairs to a number of hospitals, as long as patient health and safety were protected. On the spot, I also approved various changes in the use of facilities, such as using caesarean-section surgery rooms for ambulatory surgery, using obstetrics wards for regular medical beds, and using trailers for staff physician use.

To speed the recovery, I gave top priority to hospital repairs and directed OSHPD to delay work on all other projects not directly related to damage caused by the earthquake. Normally, before any hospital construction, renovation or repair can begin, final building plans must be approved by OSHPD, and all required fees paid.

We allowed interim non-structural repairs to begin without formal submission of plans and fees. OSHPD architects, engineers and inspectors worked on-site with the hospitals to inspect as they built -- answering questions, resolving technical problems, and advising on the development of permanent repairs.

We estimate this flexibility saved some facilities millions of dollars and several months in repair time, speeding the delivery of health care services to the community.

The Department of Health Services also worked with facilities to place beds "in suspense" instead of de-licensing unusable beds. This preserves the number of beds for which facilities are licensed and speeds the return to full operation once repairs are completed.

Recognizing the severe cash flow problems faced by damaged hospitals, Governor Wilson signed legislation just ten weeks after the quake providing relief. SB 1234 allows hospitals submitting plans for more permanent repairs to defer payment of plan review fees until they receive FEMA reimbursements. In addition, we requested the State Controller's office to assist hospitals with their FEMA applications to make the process easier.

Along with supporting the recovery process, we are working hard on several fronts to prepare for the next earthquake, including looking at the whole health care system.

The Hospital Seismic Safety Act of 1983 requires pre-1973 health care facilities to be built to a much stricter code -- one-and-one-half [1.5] times safer than all other buildings.

However, this law applied only to new hospital construction or voluntary alterations and upgrades of older hospitals. It was not retroactively applied to pre-1973 hospitals across the board.

When this 1983 Act became law, we envisioned that nonconforming hospital buildings would be replaced with new facilities through attrition. However, 20 years later, there are many older hospital buildings still in use. The Northridge quake demonstrated that hospitals built to the stricter codes suffered little damage, while several built earlier were heavily damaged.

As a result, the Governor signed SB 1953, which created a program to bring nonconforming hospital buildings into compliance with the Seismic Safety Act. Almost all acute-care hospitals in the state are included, since these facilities should be able to provide medical care to the general public after a disaster.

The legislation provides for a five-year evaluation and planning phase for hospitals, and a compliance phase that ends no later than January 1, 2030. This allows a reasonable time frame for hospitals to retrofit, replace, or change the use of existing buildings which either house patients and provide acute care or provide emergency services to the public following an earthquake.

These new laws and regulations are designed to ensure that hospitals are built and maintained at a higher safety standard so they can continue providing service to both inpatients and the community after an earthquake. This legislation will insure that older hospital buildings are brought up to more stringent safety standards, changed to non-acute care, or demolished.

We know this imposes a substantial cost on hospitals. That's why we incorporated a long compliance time frame. Despite the costs, the hospital industry supports improving the safety of older buildings. We believe this new law is good public policy.

We are interested in what you think about how best to meet the goals of this legislation, so OSHPD will be holding public meetings on February 15 and 16 to hear your suggestions. If you are interested, we have flyers available with all the information you will need.

Now, I want to shift gears and talk a bit about health care reform and where it's going in California.

Health care reform is still a major concern for the Administration. And I am so glad to be representing Pete Wilson in this debate, because he stands firmly on the side of balancing the need for health care reform with the need to create and protect jobs both here in California and throughout the nation.

Despite a spirited debate over health care reform in Washington, D.C., comprehensive health care reform has not yet been adopted by Congress. And Health Secretary Donna Shalala has said the Clinton Administration will try a "shrewder" approach to health care reform in 1995.

We have to wonder: Will the President assemble a vehicle of reform that keeps California moving in a positive direction or one that slams the brakes on our efforts to improve the health of our citizens and our economy?

Although the answer remains to be seen, California does not need and cannot afford any prescribed "solution" that eliminates our successes in addressing health care problems and contributes to our State's economic woes.

The truth is, changes are already under way in California to make health care coverage more affordable, available, and secure.

Governor Pete Wilson and I believe that we ought to fix what needs fixing, but not destroy what's working. We need to target uninsured Californians, not completely dispose of the entire health care system. We feel California is already light-years ahead of the game in reaching these uninsured people.

Let me tell you the areas in which the Governor supports provisions of the health care debate: He supports managed care, insurance reform and tort reform, and movement to primary and preventive care.

California is already implementing much of what Capitol Hill was debating, though ours, unlike Washington's, is an approach which emphasizes reform before regulation.

For example, central to nearly all Congressional proposals was managed care -organized health care delivery systems that promote access to preventive and primary care. California already has over 50 percent of its population enrolled in managed care plans, and the State has followed the private sector's lead by accelerating the enrollment of Medi-Cal recipients in managed care programs.

When California's Medi-Cal reforms in this area are fully implemented, half of the State's five million-plus Medi-Cal recipients will have made the transition to a managed care system, a move that offers improved access and quality for Medi-Cal recipients and long-term cost containment for state taxpayers.

California is leading the nation in the move towards managed care -- a move which means reorganization for many health care providers. Change is never comfortable, and it is certainly not easy. But in the midst of it all, it is important to focus on the end result: delivering the best quality health care to the most people at the lowest cost.

Insurance reform was another critical element of proposed federal change. But while Congress debated, California implemented. Pete Wilson took the initiative, and under his leadership, California is demonstrating that insurance reform can make health care coverage more affordable and available for small employers in a number of ways:

- Pooled Purchasing: California has the nation's first statewide insurance pool, the Health Insurance Plan of California (HIPC), which allows businesses to pool their purchasing power to access affordable, high-quality coverage.

  In slightly over a year of operation, the appeal of quality health products at affordable rates has attracted over 70,000 employees and dependents to the HIPC and 4,500 employers -- many of whom were previously uninsured.

Rates in the first year, which were up to 15 percent below the market, were further reduced by an average of 6.3 percent beginning in June.

And the coverage that is offered through the HIPC is of top quality -- comprehensive care which includes inpatient and outpatient care; prescription drugs; alcohol, drug, and mental health services; and dental services.

- Insurance reform: To prevent "cherry picking" whereby insurance carriers avoid certain employer groups or occupations due to health risk, California has enacted some of the most aggressive insurance reforms in the nation for the small employer market serving firms with 3 to 50 employees.

  It is important to note that the majority of California's health insurance problem is with small employers with less than 50 employees.

  Under California's reforms, small businesses are now guaranteed the issuance and renewal of insurance coverage; rate setting based on health conditions has been strictly limited to prevent dramatic premium fluctuations; preexisting condition exclusion periods have been limited to six months; and coverage has been made more "portable" to make it easier for an individual to carry coverage from one job to the next.

- Medical Malpractice: Not one Federal Plan dealt with medical malpractice. But already here in California, we have the Medical Injury Compensation Reform Act (MICRA) which puts a lid on malpractice rates doctors pay, as well as on the damages if you sue. The Governor believes any reform plan should deal with the issue of medical malpractice and not weaken MICRA's provisions.

Prevention and primary care is another component of reform discussions and have been central to Governor Wilson's strategy. In California we are targeting key populations to promote primary and preventive care.

We are expanding our Access for Infants and Mothers (AIM) program which provides affordable state-sponsored private health insurance for low-income uninsured pregnant women and their babies.

The Governor is also launching Reaching Early Access for Child Health (California REACH), a new state-supported health insurance program offering expanded access to primary and preventive health care to low-income uninsured children aged five and younger.

We do not want reforms that would mean abandoning these market-based approaches in favor of a tax-based, government-administered health system. Federal reform plans didn't guarantee that we can continue these types of programs. And preventive care provides well-documented savings -- in terms of both costs and lives.

Federal reform, if not properly done, could derail not only our current successes in health care, but our economy and state budget as well. We must keep a keen eye on the impacts federal approaches would have on California.

For example, federal proposals would have financed health care reform by imposing new mandates on the business community and levying new taxes. And President Clinton still has not decided if employer mandates will be part of his health care reform proposals this year.

Governor Wilson is vehemently opposed to employer mandates. The biggest provider of jobs in California is small business. The Governor is concerned that the health care mandate could be the final nail in the coffin, putting small businesses out of business.

The Governor's Office of Planning and Research estimated California's job losses from the employer mandate in the Clinton Plan and similar proposals would have been between 475,000 and 650,000 jobs through 1998. This level of job loss to

California is greater than the losses California has suffered to date with federal military base closures.

The State's budget was also at serious risk under the Federal Plans. Our analysis of these plans indicates that California's budget would have faced billions in increased costs between 1996 and the turn of the century because of new state spending obligations mandated by the Federal Government on the State for Medi-Cal and for long-term and community-based care.

While the goals of the federal proposals were commendable, none recognized their impact on California's fragile state budget. In crafting any future national health care reform proposals, the President must understand that California simply cannot absorb such far-reaching new mandates.

And at a time when we are working to streamline and reduce the size of government, the Federal Plans would have created new bureaucracies to oversee or "manage" California's Health Care economy, as opposed to establishing the ground rules for competition and enforcing a level playing field among the various parts of the Health Care System.

Finally, the plans advanced by the President and others ignored the escalating costs borne by California taxpayers to provide medical services to illegal immigrants -- services we're required to render under federal law.

I was shocked to learn that in five years Medi-Cal expenditures for illegal immigrants have risen from roughly $50 million to $800 million -- a 15-fold increase! And the cumulative cost of providing health care for illegals will be over $2 billion from 1988 to 1996.

In addition, 40 percent of all Medi-Cal births are to illegal immigrants. Since 1989, illegal immigrant women in California have given birth to over 217,000 babies. During this time, the demand for prenatal care for illegal immigrants drove state Medi-Cal spending for prenatal care from $17.7 million to $84 million -- a 360 percent increase in just a few years!

We have nearly 2 million illegal immigrants living in our state. For national health care reform to work in and for California, the

Federal Government must be fiscally responsible for its failure to control the border.

Reform of our nation's health care system is essential to address the lack of coverage for our nation's uninsured, improve efficiency and contain costs, and promote the delivery of quality care. But reform of our system must be pragmatic and undertaken in the context of our economic climate.

Mandatory "solutions" that would cripple California's economic recovery are not responsible solutions to our health coverage problems.

Rather, market-based solutions which establish fair market rules, create incentives for the delivery of timely, cost-effective care, and offer strategies such as pooled purchasing to provide additional options for consumers which enhance competition, can serve as the foundation for reform.

They are the foundation of efforts here in California -- efforts which are successfully expanding health coverage, stabilizing and reducing the cost of coverage, preventing new costs to government and promoting a warm climate for job creation.

Thank you. Now I'd like to open it up for questions.

QUESTIONS AND ANSWERS

QUESTION: Yes. I consider myself a friend of the governor's, but I'm very concerned on a point you know an issue you didn't mention in funding all these hospitals to rebuild after the earthquake, we're supposed to be closing down 50% of the hospitals over the next couple of years by the normal mandates here. Why are we funding on the one hand to build and make capital improvements which is just lost money to the taxpayers?

ANSWER: Well in all instances, I think I can say "all," they dramatically downsize. I know in the case of St. John's, they downsized. I don't think anybody builds to the amount that they were building. They built to a much lesser amount. And I think they definitely understood that they had an over-beddage situation here in the L.A. basin, but I think that was taken into consideration as to the size of the facility they rebuilt. You know, I'd be interested in hearing if you think that's not true and if you still think there are too many beds here in the L.A. basin. You're shaking your head "yes"? There are too many? Or? What? What are you saying?

QUESTION: I think most of us would agree there are too many. I'm not trying to put the tap, but I think you have to be much more careful on where the money goes because you know it is a loss of certain resources. That's, you know, between the Cal Mortgage program, and I think you know that . . .

ANSWER: Right.

QUESTION: . . . the administration would have nothing to do with it.

ANSWER: And how are we going to pay for the body impediments and all of that when there are hospitals that are already funded? Yes?

QUESTION: Do you foresee more legislation to be necessary to get more limits in California?

ANSWER: No. And we're seeing the private companies start to get this, and they're successful. And the Governor certainly wants to encourage that as a market with a market-based solution to health care. Yes?

QUESTION: I first want to congratulate you for the work you did. You're in a rough work experience. For those of you who are not familiar with what she did, she was there at the time, to make sure - people had health care --

ANSWER: Thank you.

QUESTION: Recently the *L.A. Times* has brought out a series of articles criticizing some of the hospitals that have been given permission to stay operational.

ANSWER: The Governor felt that this needed to be done. And it's going to be an interesting thing since he's appointed some of those members on the Seismic Safety Commission that are coming out with this verdict. And obviously the Governor did not want any patient safety problems. I mean, he said to do everything within the context of safety. But working with the hospitals, I felt very assured. They're not going to put patients in peril. They don't want to open their doors and have a calamity. And we had people right on that time, and I was very assured that what we did, I felt very good about it. And I don't think we put anybody in peril, and I was at Holy Cross four and five times during that. I got in the day after the temblor. That was the biggest thing I've ever been in, uh, a little bit scary. You know I just simply do not agree that our people misjudged the facts, and they are structurally sound now. Nobody was in peril. They were saying that if they had another earthquake they might have been in peril. I think it's a difference of opinion, and I think the Seismic Safety Commission tends to be a bit more overconservative than I think really needs to be. And I don't feel that I put anybody in peril with the decisions I made. Okay. Sir?

QUESTION: Is there any kind of analysis being done or has it been done on the solvency of other hospitals where they've gotten more in insurance, because we've talked a lot about that, about the reason a bond issue may be in jeopardy over that spot.

ANSWER: Right. Cal Mortgage has had a couple of tough situations lately, and I think they are cognizant of that. I think that definitely is part of what they're looking at, but you know it's really tough. I was telling Sherwin about a call from a friend in Ventura, and they were saying that the hospital of Ventura was losing patients and yet the county was going to come in and build a whole new wing and a whole new county hospital. And he was saying, "Wait a minute, there are existing hospitals, why are we funding these new ones?" And why are we building these huge" . . . and I guess you were telling me about one in San Bernardino also. And that is a problem. And I think that does need to be looked at. I'm going to just look into this thing for my friend in Ventura because it seems ridiculous that we're building with taxpayer money county hospitals, when you have sufficient local hospitals, and I think that -- but as I said earlier, we're in a huge change and it's tough for everybody. The docs are upset about managed care, and the specialists are upset about managed care -- a big change. And so it's going to take a lot, and I think this kind of a group is terrific because you have all aspects represented here, and I think some good things will probably come out of your meeting. And we need help up there, and anything you have to offer I'd really like to hear from you. Yes?

QUESTION: I heard you say that facilities will have to over the year 2030 to come into compliance?

ANSWER: Right.

QUESTION: I think CalTech says there's something like a very high probability of a major quake in the next 10 or 15 years.

ANSWER: Well, what do you do in a situation like this? Do you put hospitals out of business, forcing them to retrofit in a time frame that's not realistic? And I say "no" and I think we need to give them this time in order for them to remain economically viable and that's the direction we're going now. Tell me, you know, how you disagree and what would you do -- on the one hand -- put a hospital out and not have them deal or afford to make those repairs? And I guess what we were trying to come up with was a logical meeting of the minds and saying, "Well, what would work, what are you realistically able to do?" And that's what they came up with.

QUESTION: There are already a lot of illegal aliens that slipped through the net I think on Medicaid, so I'm wondering what's going to happen if Proposition 187 will get enacted; what's the Governor's position on getting some financial reimbursement to providers that are going to wind up taking care of this group?

ANSWER: Well, we know the Governor has put in for reimbursement for illegal immigration. It's not looking just terrific. We're getting a sympathetic ear with the new Congress. It's more sympathy and wanting to change and beef up the border than actually giving us any money. And we have about $732 million built into this budget counting on reimbursement, and we're probably going to get about half of that. And we probably could manage what we have here now. What we can't manage is the unknown of how many will come tomorrow or next week. And that's what we're saying to the Federal Government. Patrol the border. Stop it. And they did that. They did a huge assault on El Paso and cut the number by 75%, and look what they did in the Cuban crisis. They sent 4,000 Coast Guard and Navy to help interrupt in a situation in Florida that was going on for a month, and they were getting -- horrors! -- 5 to a 1,000 per day for a month. We've had 1,500-3,000 a day for multiple months and where were our 4,000 Navy and Coast Guard to close our border? That's Pete Wilson's issue: patrol the border, keep them from coming in the first place, and we'll manage what's here.

CAPITAL FORMATION IN THE 1990s

Restructures, Workouts & Reorganizations

CAPITAL FORMATION IN THE 1990s

Restructures, Workouts, Reorganizations

Every health care facility audit solution will require some amount of capital. Except in the rare and envious case where adequate capital is already on hand, capital formation will also be required. In this Part III, we discuss:

☐ **Kinds.** There are basically two kinds of capital, "debt" and "equity." All capital investment requires risk and expects reward. The difference between debt and equity capital is the difference in their risk and reward characteristics. Debt takes priority over equity, accepts less risk than equity, at least in theory, and commands less potential for reward than equity. Whether debt or equity, all capital formation requires some identification and appropriate application.

☐ **Debt.** What changes have occurred and are occurring in debt financing? Why? Who is lending today? What is actually available? Where? What are the terms? "Equity kickers?" Taxable? Tax exempt? What are the current underwriting standards and criteria? Credit enhancement. Structuring and preparing the loan application.

☐ **Equity.** Who is investing today? Terms? Structures? Criteria? Structuring and preparing the "application"/"offering." Federal and state "securities" law disclosure requirements.

☐ **Reorganization and Workouts.** The 1980s "stepchild" comes of 1990s age, and legitimacy. Recognizing signs of the "troubled" entity. Overview of bankruptcy law -- Chapter 7 "liquidations" and Chapter 11 "reorganizations." "Workouts" outside bankruptcy. Bankruptcy financing. Special health care considerations, including government receivables.

BARAK: The planning session that we're coming to right now concerns capital formation and capital reorganization. I suspect it doesn't come as a surprise to anyone in this room that the '90s represent different set of capital formation challenges than in the past.

When we talk about "capital," we need to make sure that we're all using the same terminology. There are two primary kinds of capital; "equity" and "debt." Equity refers to the interest, or the value, or the investment, of the owners. They're the ones who aren't sure what their yield will be, but know where they stand, at the back of the line. At least in theory, debt takes less risk, but also enjoys less upside.

Historically, owners ran into troubles on their debt because they were without the revenue to service the debt and the loans fell into default. In the '90s, we're often experiencing a very difficult kind of loan default. Values have dropped, but underwriting standards have gone up. So, today, you very often find someone in a credit crunch not because they can't service the debt that confronts them, but because the debt is maturing or is about to mature and they can't find any available refinancing.

Track record notwithstanding, underwriters don't want to exacerbate the problems they've suffered elsewhere. Increased equity is often the only solution today, but that's not available in unlimited supply either.

All of these challenges lead to somewhat of a stepchild, "Chapter 11" Bankruptcy reorganization is very much emerging in the '90s and is probably anything but a stepchild today. With that, I turn the podium back to Sherwin, who will introduce our third panel and get us under way.

MEMEL: People who are going to speak to you on this panel have had a tremendous amount of experience in dealing with reorganizations, with financing and refinancing and examining these organizations very carefully with their future.
The speakers will be Bryan Marsal, who's a founding managing director of Alvarez & Marsal and since 1983 has been involved in providing financial operational services to the public. One of Bryan's claims to fame is having taken Republic out of Chapter 11 and turning it around. That's only one of the turnarounds that Bryan has done. Incidentally, he's, an alumnus of Citibank as is Al Smith who is now Senior Vice President of GE Capital Corporation in Dallas, Texas.

Al is involved in health care lending at GE Capital; before that, he was responsible for one of the three health care origination teams in Citibank, managing asset portfolios in excess of $500,000,000 and has a long distinguished career in banking, specializing in the health care field.

Charlie Plimpton joins us today from nearby Irvine, California, where he's vice president of the health care group in the investment banking division of NUVEEN and his responsibilities include finance and advisory services to some of the major health care organizations including Banking Franciscan Services, Toronto Left Health Systems; Sisters of Charity of Nazareth. I think the important thing is divining the work he's been responsible for since 1990. He served as the lead banker for 22 health care bond issues totaling over a billion dollars in hard value financing.

Simon Aron is my partner. He is chairman of the bankruptcy and creditors right department in the law firm of Manatt, Phelps & Phillips. His practice involves all aspects of bankruptcy and creditor rights with a particular emphasis on commercial transactions, workouts and reorganizations. He's an accomplished trial practitioner and lectures in numerous bar associations and other organizations. And when I'm in trouble I call him for help! On behalf of my clients, that is!

Our final speaker on this panel is Craig L. McKnight, whom I've known for years. He is one of the leaders in health care financing and consulting and accounting in the country. Prior to transferring to Philadelphia this past June, he was the senior partner in charge of the Los Angeles office service industry practice which include ecology, universities and nonprofit and governmental health care practices. His clients are the Who's Who In Healthcare. He's had tremendous experience in managed care along with his clients Stanford University Hospital, Blue Cross of California, Beverly Enterprises, Maxicare Healthcare claims.

This is very distinguished panel. I'd like to call Bryan Marsal to begin.

Bryan P. Marsal
Alvarez & Marsal, Inc.
New York, NY

MARSAL: Thank you. My name is Bryan Marsal. I am one of the notorious black and white polite new candidates that you might have read about. I specialize in bankruptcy with regard to recovering companies. The health care industry has been very fertile ground for me in the last 8 years. I fully expect that in the next 10 years it will be better than in the last 8 in this region.

Oftentimes the topic is capital formation. What I'd like is to make the point that most of my clients come to me with their requests, saying to me, "Bryan, what do I do? How do I restructure myself?" What they're really asking is "Bryan, can you get me cheap money? Can you get me a way to deal with my bank problems, with my insurance company problems, and with my note problems?" My response to every one of those clients is always the same: that potential restructuring is really a second step.

Financial restructuring are the clothes that are worn on the body. The body is the operational structure, the operating plan. It never ceases to amaze me how many people fail to understand they have to take a hard look at themselves operationally.

My second question to the client is, "I just don't understand. GNP indicators suggest that health care is getting a greater and greater portion of the gross national product. I don't understand why you -- and these tend to be professionally possible providers -- "I don't understand why with a growing market like that you're singing this `woe is me' operational tune." What I ask them to do is describe their problems, and my conclusion very quickly is: "You're not coping with change very well, Mr. Hospital Administrator."

If I'm not fired at that point, usually we go to the next step. I tell my client that the first step is to stop thinking of himself or herself as a hospital. That's the first problem you're having. You're not a hospital; you're a provider of health care services. A provider of health care services controls outpatient delivery, whether it be diagnostic or surgical. Judy said in her presentation earlier, "My God, how those hospitals have lost market share." I tell my clients what would you do if you were the down end provider in the market. What you forbid to have happen is you forbid all these outpatient competitors to come here and eat your lunch. Now you're coming to me and saying "woe is me because I can't do business?"

Invariably, from the hospital health care industry I get altruistic motives. I said "that's enough." Your basic objective is to first deliver a customer, and stop thinking of your patient as a patient, and start thinking of him as a customer. Think of yourself as being a customer-friendly, cost-effective quality health care product. Leave all the rest of that nonsense at the door. You know, this is nonsense. It's not for-profit nonsense. You're in a business, my friend, and you have to compete. You have to compete, and you are fighting for your life right now, because you're so late getting started. Again, if I'm still employed, I say, "Let's take a look at your business and do an operational audit. A very quick operational audit." Your business is like no other business in this country, even though every one of you out there in the health care industry believe that you're distinctly different, you're really not as far as one of my clients. There are three basic functions: First, there's a sales/marketing function. Second, there's a production/distribution function. Third, there's a finance function. Do an honest operational assessment of yourself and your capabilities. On the sales front, who's your customer, what do you define as customer service? That isn't what customer service is about. Customer service is a relationship in the future between your facility, between you and the customer; that patient. That's the only way you're going to do business. In fact, in one instance, I was sent from Dallas to Disney World. From Miami Hospital, I said why don't you go to Disney World? I want you to see what customer service is about.

It's really very important because I think most of the people you help here are intrigued; a doctor, a nurse, a hospital administrator. God bless you out there, and you think of yourselves as "caregivers." However, the patient is the beneficiary of your good will. The patient becomes the customer. That's what has to change in this industry. Most of those of you who are going to succeed are going to change that customer caliber.

The second point is production. Production is the newsroom, and you look at your facility production. Well, what's production? I pass through excess capacity. You can't pass through excess capacity. That's your problem. What do I do? Either you become a parking lot or your competitor across the street becomes a parking lot, because you have too much production capacity here. That's what we can do if we were making tires. That's what we would do in any other business. So why not in health care? This is because health care is a very personal thing to us; we MUST find a sure-fire way to make it personal. I heard one of the earlier speakers talking about distribution. I disagree that the nexus of the hospital system is going to change in the next 10 years. I think the hospitals are simply a component of the health care delivery system. They are not the cornerstone; they are not the center of the Universe concept; they won't be in the future. Technology has gone beyond that.

What you're going to have is the customer wanting convenient, quick in-and-out service, similar to what you want when you walk into McDonald's or Burger King. That's what health care is becoming. If you want to find the truth, we did a survey of our patients, and the two things they dreaded the most were going to the Department of Motor Vehicles and checking into the hospital. This is scary but true. The consumer was telling you that is the last thing we want to do because it's very painful and time-consuming.

Regarding distribution, I think what you're going to have in the future are outpatient delivery systems. You're going to have clinics located nearby in the community, and you're going to have a hospital only as a cost-effective convenient place to bring most patients who are not at a critical mass at your location.

The final function I want to focus on is finance. People do what they know how to do and that's the continuation from TRV days.

Now we say, "But that's over 10 years ago; we've gotten out of that." Now we use these grandiose schemes like FTEs and patient for a day.

On the financial side of things, we need product line, and service line, out the door. Your best tools are business as usual. Those are the tools that the hospital and the health care industry need to have, and they don't have that. Most of you don't have that. In addition, what you're going to need are outcome and diagnostic studies because a consumer is going to base the first decision on what you say first.

My mother's going to come to a hospital or come to a facility because service is quick and the food is hot. She doesn't have a clue as to what the cardiology statistics are or whether or not there's good or bad health care here; she's going to let that, she's going to leave that decision to somebody else. I really believe that you're going to need those statistics in order to market effectively to the insurance payor.

The human resource assessment is important because even as we run this operation, you have to have horses to play this game. Then that is when I usually tell my client if you have enough horses to play this game, acknowledge them; there are some people who just are not going to change. If you're not going to cope with the new change, then sell out to somebody who is. The value is not going to go up. In fact, Sherwin is the new client to whom I gave this speech. Sell out now because the values are going to go down.

I don't view the health care industry as in a state of decline. Quite the contrary. I view it in a state of change. It's in a lot of flux. I view that as being relevant. I think it's a business that needs lots of money and opportunity. However, the bottom line is quit feeling sorry for yourself if you happen to be in that mode. Either get competitive or get out of the business. That's it.

Charles G. Plimpton
John Nuveen & Co., Incorporated
Irvine, CA

PLIMPTON: Good afternoon, Sherwin Memel, Al Smith and others. Al's been working primarily with proprietary in the last few years. Sherwin is wise because he knows that Al and I are coming closer and closer on bringing together the fork in the middle of the street, not necessarily because the proprietaries are winning the battle of the health care setting. One could really argue, as Bryan said, that values are very high right now, and the proprietaries are truly a greater pool. What's really happening is that the power of health care delivery is changing. Capital is flowing out of traditional hospital settings into different venues of care. We have to try to track that.

My comments were taken from a document that was obtained in the syllabus; it was under Al's materials, and his outline and my outline are together. I want to admit to you right now that this is entirely appropriate because I was taught always to respect my elders. I would like to talk about the flow of our business and how it is similar to what Al is doing. I have to echo his comments, and I've underscored them many times.

It is a cash flow business; it is not an asset business. Tax-exempt financing has been reserved as you all know from proprietary organizations. There are tax-exempt legislation or regulations in patient care. There is an increasing concentration of buying power amongst tax-exempt pools of money. This is deemed to be a retail sector. What we have now is a market where the response institutionally is to situations. There really is no distinction or very little distinction between private placement, where you're negotiating specifically with our two liners, and broad retail public offering. The standards and the climbers tend to be the same.

Tax-exempts remain ridiculously low-cost forms of life. If you buy insurance with AAA, your long-term rate will be somewhat in the area of 88% of the United States government, which is a very favorable rate. If your rate will tend to be involved in the short municipal market, and the variable rate market, their rates will tend to be something like 72%. This is very attractive, but again there's adaptation of the industry and movement of capital out of hospitals from different sources. On the taxable side, hospitals have tried to find placement of monies through pension funds, insurance companies, commercial mortgage companies, and banks. The parameters remain the same, but as you all know, collateral values have collapsed, and the lending values that are communicated to us would suggest that lenders right now are making extreme promises. Fifty percent of the total debt-to-collateral ratio are working under coverage ratios in the area of 1-1/2 times, and much more stringently than we saw even 10 years ago. I think we all understand this is happening because values have dropped, but increasingly you will see it become less important as the cash flow gains in substance. We're beginning to see a taxable market right now, that is built upon retail once again, but here it's a different type of retail, much more fragmented if you have the credit. There is municipal bond assurance or if you have sufficient rating you can make a public offering of taxable bonds even though you represent a credit that is relatively unfamiliar to the other normal attachable buyers. We're seeing this certainly in the case of hospitals that are using this in financing position acquisitions or practice acquisitions; we're also seeing position groups themselves begin to access taxable monies at extremely favorable rates, both long and short. The sum and substance underscoring what you're seeing is a fragmentation of the business that is breaking down intó its components, and capital is following this. In the last page, right before tab 6, you referred to some of the cutter ratios have been acknowledged for triple-B equivalents in the different components, and nursing homes, hospitals, kitchen halls, and the like. This is what the market now is beginning to rely on in terms of credit standards, and this emphasis continues to be going concern. What is the government? What is the management? What is the new location? How many lines? Those are the instruments of credit management and investment decisions that are now in our market. Thank you very much for your time.

Simon Aron, Esq.
Manatt, Phelps & Phillips
Los Angeles, CA

ARON: I am Simon Aron, a member of Manatt, Phelps & Phillips and head of the Firm's Bankruptcy and Creditors' Rights Department. Just yesterday I was having a conversation with a colleague who was an attorney and is today an investment banker working with troubled companies and the conversation turned to vultures. Now, once upon a time - in financial circles - this was an unfriendly term used to describe opportunistic "birds of prey" who pick over the leftovers of troubled companies and liquidate them for scrap value. Recently "vulture" funds are all in vogue. Several prominent investment houses have established their own vulture funds.

Today, terms such as bankruptcy, debtor, bankrupt, insolvency and reorganization still have negative connotations, but have become terms of art and with the recession of the last few years fairly commonplace in business and financial circles.

Almost with the beginning of the new decade came deflation and the need for restructuring of the massive amounts of debt accumulated in the "go-go 80s." In our context this means the deceleration of leveraged assets and the restructuring of business operations. The hoped-for result is the return of the enterprise to profitability and a return to the creditors and equity holders who have invested their money in the enterprise.

Reorganizations under Chapter 11 have become a powerful tool available to all of the parties in the pursuit of these results. What I would like to walk you through is what this tool can mean to a financially distressed company. For example, it is a way of implementing the ideas and strategies that Bryan Marsal was just discussing. It may also be used to protect junior creditors and shareholders from aggressive enforcement actions by senior creditors.

First, let me give you a little background. In 1979, there was enacted the first truly curative reorganization bankruptcy statute for general consumption. Underlying the drafter's intent behind Chapter 11 was a very simple concept, which on more than one occasion I have articulated to a judge in a courtroom as follows: insolvent does not mean without value. In bankruptcy, "insolvent" may mean balance sheet insolvency -- meaning one's liabilities exceed the value of one's assets, or cash flow insolvent which means that one cannot pay its debts as they mature in the ordinary course. However, the bankruptcy statute, as enacted does not require that the company or the "debtor" be insolvent in order to reorganize or liquidate. So, for example, everyone may remember that Texaco filed for Chapter 11 relief although it was never "insolvent."

What was intended by the Bankruptcy Code is to provide a forum for the troubled or "insolvent" company to reorganize around the core value or operations of an insolvent enterprise. If successfully reorganized, creditors, shareholders and business markets in general would benefit more than by liquidation of the bricks and mortar. Furthermore, the reorganization would benefit society as a whole through the preservation of jobs and the production and consumption of goods and services by the reorganized entity through the continuation of a business or enterprise that might otherwise disappear.

Shortly after the enactment of Chapter 11 Bankruptcy Code in 1979, many of us saw truly splendid examples of what could be accomplished under this reorganization statute. On the West Coast, many of you may recall Wickes going through Chapter 11 and the turnaround and success that enterprise had in the early to mid-80s. As the years have passed, the stigma associated with the bankrupt or insolvent debtor lessened and I look at them as being analogous to the bitter aftertaste one gets from a diet soda. Moreover, bankruptcy and reorganization have also become words associated with opportunity.

That is not to say that the key to success is to find insolvency or by becoming bankrupt. Rather, I think it has become uniformly acknowledged that reorganization, restructuring and bankruptcy are accepted business strategies, as well as a powerful business too.

Turning to the reorganization process, Chapter 11 envisions a conceptually level playing field between the troubled company and enterprise and its managers and operators, and its creditors both secured and unsecured -- whether as secured lender, bondholder, trade or other creditor -- and public or private shareholders or partners -- the equity holders. And in bankruptcy more than any other context we see often the immediate conversion of debt to equity and equity to spectators. But spectators who often have the ability to influence the outcome of the proceedings because the basis for the level playing field is that each of these constituents has rights against the others. In fact, it is often the recalcitrant party that turns out to be the big loser. Because bankruptcy provides a forum or arena and a supervised opportunity to reach an agreement between the troubled enterprise and its managers and employees, and its creditors and shareholders. This agreement forms the basic plan for the financial reorganization of the company and allows for the operational reorganization of the enterprise.

In subsequent years a consensus developed and has been published through the last few years, in particular, that this level playing field has become or always was disproportionately slanted in favor of the debtor and reorganization. The legislative response to this consensus was a balancing act that recently was enacted in the Bankruptcy Reform Act of 1994. The materials I have provided you today hopefully will give you some background and insight into the changes to Chapter 11 in the 1994 Act. Some of the provisions of the 1994 Act are also summarized there.

Although I get involved in many health care and real estate cases, including some health care-real estate cases, I do not consider myself a real estate or health care expert. Rather, I look at my job much like I imagine a mechanic would: focusing on isolating problems and developing bankruptcy or other legal solutions that implement the business decisions necessary to capitalize on the value of the distressed enterprise. The process of restructuring and reorganizing through Chapter 11 hopefully allows the health care enterprise in financial trouble to deal with the existing real estate or operational crisis, while preserving the enterprise and the jobs and services connected thereto. Applying this powerful business tool to the issues, crisis, and possible solutions I have heard today from the other panelists and audience participants, a few items occurred to me that should be passed on:

First of all, the process of reorganizing through bankruptcy must be carefully considered and weighed against other alternatives; it is most effective when thoroughly planned, detailed and approached after a plan or strategy has been developed. In considering the many aspects of health care crisis discussed here today, it seems that most people agree that demand for services is growing faster than the rate of inflation, and thus the question becomes how to capitalize on this particular demand and, potentially at the same time, deal with the over leveraged or outdated existing enterprise. And to follow what Bryan Marsal said, stop thinking of yourselves as "hospitals," but think of yourselves as providing products and services to consumers.

In contrast to the planned, measured approach, a good many situations are responses to negative operating results and the projection of continuing negative results and sudden conclusions by creditors or management that a problem exists or that the company is caught in a downward spiral of increasing financial strain. These situations often result in a quick but unfortunate decision to rush into a bankruptcy alternative, where other alternatives exist. Those other alternatives may not involve bankruptcy or only the threat of bankruptcy, or a pre-packaged plan of reorganization. Workouts and consensual restructurings are alternatives to be explored before the bankruptcy petition is filed. Such consensual, out of court arrangements have been very common occurrences over the last two-three years. However, these alternatives inevitably require time and can be solicited only with regard to the problems and the potential for reorganization.

Carter Hawley Hale and other cases we have heard about have resulted in successful Chapter 11 reorganizations. A greater number even have resulted over recent years in successful out of court workouts and restructurings. It seems to me that you in hospitals or the health care industry are suffering from essentially a catch-22 -- between cash demands of their real estate holdings, downsizing, repairing and maintaining facilities, and the costs and liabilities associated with the need for better technology, equipment, and personnel to service and capitalize on the increased demand for services. This effect is again one that you will hear from Brain and from Craig McKnight, whom you will be hearing from shortly, can address in designing business strategies that can be implemented by and through negotiations and out of courts resolutions, or through court-supervised proceedings under Chapter 11. Thank you.

Albert E. Smith
General Electric Capital Corporation
Dallas, TX

SMITH: Thank you. I want to keep this short and hopefully, thought provoking. After lunch one of the few alternatives available to a speaker is the creative use of hand grenades. I may be rolling one into this crowd when I tell you that I don't believe funding strategies ought to be based on the real estate assets a firm possesses or on its other tangible assets, unless it has no alternative. If the asset pool is driving Debt Capacity, that is a situation you should endeavor to change. What should be driving an enterprise's value and its debt capacity is its cash flow and where you are taking that cash flow. The economic value of any business comes from its future cash flows; assets which do not produce positive cash flow may have no value. Investors, lenders and buyers will examine a business's cash flow for dependability, growth prospects, and how it might affect cash flows they want to join to it.

In 1993, I had the distinct pleasure to advise Fountain Valley and Mission Viejo Hospitals as they separately explored various sale opportunities. As usual, beauty was in the eye of the beholder. The historic cash flows set a floor value that a buyer could expect to gain with prudent management. The final values, however, were determined by how the buyers perceived the hospitals would enhance the cash flows of their existing regional networks. OrNda, for example, needed a tertiary care hospital to complement and complete its network of lower intensity hospitals in Orange County. In this case, the analysis of value was based on a sophisticated projection of combined future cash flows and not on a simple appraisal based examination of assets.

If you are going to be involved in capital formation for your business, you need to be intimately aware of how the capital markets determine value and debt capacity.

Value of course, can be determined based on a number of well established methodologies such as discounted cash flow, public company market valuations (which can be used to calculate value as a multiple of cash flow), or you can use recent comparable sales.

Equity capital sources will be primarily focused on how your business strategy takes existing value and creates additional value that does not exist today. If the owner/founder wants to share fairly in the upside with venture capital partners, he must be aware of what portion of current and future value he is giving up to obtain the equity capital.

Debt capital, on the other hand, focuses on historical cash flows and today's value. The only future cash flows that debt capital will give you credit for, in addition to those that already exist are modest inflationary increases and savings related to specific cost reductions which usually have to be in the process of implementation. Debt capital is available at the discount to the total value of the firm. In the acute care hospital industry for example, values range generally from 5 to 7 times EBITDA (Earning Before Interest, Taxes, Depreciation and Amortization). The bank debt market will generally lend up to 3.5 times EBITDA and the high yield bond market will provide additional funds up to 5 times EBITDA. Equity capital is presumed to provide the rest of the capital structure. In addition to these leverage benchmarks, the firm will also have to demonstrate interest coverage of at least 2 times and coverage of fixed charges which includes principal repayments, interest and capital expenditures of 1.25 times. These leverage and coverage tests are central to determining debt capacity. Beyond these factors management is essential, asset support is positive, size helps, regulatory intervention hurts, complexity hurts, and of course any pervasive uncertainty caused by issues like Health Care Reform is negative. The managers of any enterprise should know what the maximum debt capacity is at any time. How far they press against this debt capacity is a function of their business strategy and the financial risk they are willing to accept.

The debt capital markets will deny a company access based on cash flows if the cash flows are untested or erratic. Young companies which typically have unseasoned cash flows will need to use their assets to obtain debt capital. REITs and finance companies provide capital on this basis and many of today's sub-acute and rehab companies were built on this basis. Most of these companies will attempt at some point, to use their post rent cash flows to obtain debt on a cash flow basis.

Troubled companies may also be unable to use their cash flows due to recent discontinuities in those cash flows. These companies can sometimes obtain asset-based debt on the basis of their receivables which can be placed in a bankruptcy remote subsidiary.

Various segments of the capital markets go hot and cold just like any other business. During 1994, the Bank Syndicated Loan Market was extremely active. Most banks are now well-capitalized and in compliance with federally-mandated capital requirements. This compliance has freed them to add assets to their balance sheets. Resurgent M&A activity and refinancings have provided the volume and other capital markets have become less attractive due to rising interest rates. In 1994, the syndicated loan market increased 71% to $665 billion. In spite of this volume, competition has driven fees and interest spreads to very low levels.

For the healthcare sector, access to this market has never been better. Almost every major money center and regional bank now has a specialized healthcare department. These lenders have also broadened their activity into almost every segment of the industry. Foreign banks, also seem to have finally explained this business to their credit gurus in London, Paris, and Tokyo.

The high yield market, after very good years in 1992 and 1993, fell off in 1994 due to rising interest rates. In January, however, over $1 billion in cash flowed into the high yield mutual funds and signaled a possible easing of the market when it becomes apparent that interest rates have peaked or flattened out, access to this market will become more predictable.

Healthcare REITs which begun in the mid 80s as captive finance vehicles have reached maturity and are now well diversified and generally independent from healthcare providers. They continue to represent an important source of financing for emerging companies, but investment in the past several years seems to have been predominantly in the Long-Term Care/Sub Acute

Arena. Rising interest rates and bank competition may affect investment activity this year. Fortunately for REITs this industry is still quite fragmented.

I want to thank you. This cash flow approach to the debt and equity markets is sometimes very foreign to real estate professionals and not-for-profit managers, but I hope it has been valuable in outlining how the taxable sector is raising money and in explaining why the for-profit providers behave as they do.

Craig L. McKnight
Coopers & Lybrand
Philadelphia, PA

MCKNIGHT: Let me explain a little bit as to why we've come. There are at least five notable things missing in Philadelphia that have been an advantage. First of all we've not had a single riot, there have been no floods, no fires and no earthquakes. The one final interesting thing is that there is not nearly as much advantage here. One of the advantages to coming in late on the panel is that everybody has said it all by the time you stand up.

I had a great change in my career in the late '80s that involved some situations with MaxiCare. Some others that we were asked to take a look at, not as much for what it was yesterday, but what it is today, and more importantly, what it is tomorrow that will change my career. We had to prove to a lot of physicians that we were actually analyzing the situation from a professional standpoint. It was important to watch that it was the enterprise value that became important with restructuring and to focus on the operations going forward. But you've heard that, and normally I would spend a lot of time talking about that, but that's already been said by nearly everyone. That is clearly crucial in the restructuring.

Let me for a minute switch a little bit to something new and hopefully something that you'll find useful as restructuring goes forward. I had an interesting experience a few years ago, that I think is a similar parallel; we were asked to go back and look at one of the major churches in the world. They were being audited, and they had never been audited before. It was a learning experience for both the church and ourselves. This is one of the big questions, given the building had been built centuries ago. "What do we do for a cost basis on the real estate?" There was a lot of discussion as to how to do that. When we came back to them, we said, "We don't think the buildings are assets -- we think the buildings are liabilities."

Once we broke that water, there was a whole new discussion as to how we would look at the real estate holdings, because they were single use buildings, etc. How's this a common situation with health care? There are some regulations that date back many, many years ago to the older crowd in the room who look to cost reimbursement.

Not all of the programs reimbursed hospitals for the cost of depreciation and interest. Even when payment for patients went to other basis, that reimbursement lasted several years. As a result of that, many of us spent the early part of our careers churning hospitals. Nevertheless, it seems to be a fact that it has been going on for a long time.

The rate of the sales price of hospitals is continually going up, and as a result of that recapture policy, if a hospital is sold for more than its cost, then it depreciates. However, they would recapture that depreciation, and it would have to be paid back. They got anxious in looking at that, and there were a number of hospitals that minimize that recapture. Hospitals have expanded their regulation rules a bit more aggressively to incorporate statutory virtues and other forms of combination, and they have recovered some significant amounts of previously paid reimbursements. Now, what does all that mean? That's all history. What it means today is those regulations stayed in place.

I sit in on the CPA healthcare committee, and we entertained the issue of whether or not a hospital's unused capacity can be written down; when you look at the hospitals, it's not a very pleasant adjustment to make. When we were talking about, we had the idea that we were in the process of implementing for a number of the non-profits that are emerging today. If you look at their combination, it became the reverse of the prior days, when we were churning hospitals' increase in rates and costs of the structures.

In reality, if you look at cost accounting, when you from a number of non-profits and add them together, you have significant fund balance. It becomes the purchase price. I put calculations into the computer, and if I put them on the screen, I'll put you to sleep in a matter of seconds. Conceptually, if you take over the payments, the amount of your fund balance becomes a loss. Therefore, if you have had 50% reimbursement, when you have that loss and you reallocate the purchase price to the assets, the last assets that get any allocation are your building and equipment. By the time you get to the calculations effectively, you end up with healthcare real estate that results in a loss.

Now, to give you an example, we are currently working with two 250-bed hospitals, and non-profit facilities that are having a statutory merger. If you bought a hospital, it would be the same process. If you bought a hospital for liability, you'd have a loss of the equivalent of potential loss on that building for one hospital. When you have a statutory merger, both hospitals form a new corporation, and there is a significantly larger amount that is doubled. And for two 250-bed hospitals, and as much as we deal in non-profits throughout California, it results in a Medicare payment for the pre-stated depreciation. These are two fairly normal hospitals. We have another situation where there are five hospital facilities in the amount of over $100 million. Thus, it is an interesting source of capital. There are various hurdles that I don't have time to get into and there are some technical things to be watched.

The bottom line is there are opportunities that exist with the hospital affiliates that result in significant amounts of depreciation, that would never be reimbursed in what I call the "good ole days". It appears to be normal, but it is something relatively new with a very high chance of succeeding. We've got some hospitals who get relatively small amounts, but the larger amounts would not be readily available. The same thing happens in a restructure situation. I think the real opportunity exists here and as we look at the different non-profits and facilities, one of the things to watch for in the affiliation are changes in the disproportionate shares. Some of the other technical things are the reimbursements that actually can be beneficial by consolidating them. Be careful how you consolidate, which hospitals you bring together and which ones you don't. Significant benefits are still available through those programs. Something that you don't want to forget about are the favorable positives and the negative steps in which Bryan has had experience. So keep those in mind. I think I've covered the high points for you. If there any questions, please feel free to ask.

QUESTIONS AND ANSWERS

MEMEL: We've got about 15 minutes before our break. Before we go into the workshops I hope you'll take advantage of the tremendous talent that's with us today, and present to them your questions or what opportunities may exist in the area. I'd like to throw out a question to the panel, perhaps primarily to Bryan: What do you do when you have a situation where you have typically two 400 or 500-bed community hospitals in urban settings that are within a mile of each other, frequently with religious sponsorship, one non-profit; the other one is for profit or a community not-for-profit, but not sponsored by a religious order, and it's absolutely clear, there's no room for both of them? They've each been suffering along the way as everybody has tended to do, and they've almost reached the limit of their downsizing. You discuss the needs of the physicians in the marketplace and get called in by one of them. How do you tell them to analyze the situation and look for a future? What remedies may be available to them?

PANELIST: I will give you an example in Miami. We have two hospitals that were three miles apart, Parkway Medical owned by AMI which is about a 300-bed facility, and nearby was another for-profit, which was about the same size, and was where we did about $5 million a year in operating profits. We had two facilities in the Miami market, each one was operating on roughly 45% capacity. What we eventually did was, we went to AMI and made them an offer they couldn't refuse. They literally shut it down and made it into an office building and it didn't really matter. It could not be used for health care purposes ever again, removing that capacity from the market place. The community, for its hospital needs, had to concentrate on Parkway. The following year Parkway went from $6 million to $24 million. You cannot make money with most production facilities where your operation is at 45% capacity. The economics change very dramatically when you are able to operate at a much higher level of occupancy.

MEMEL: Are you saying that one made $6 million, the other made $5 million, and when you put them together, they made $24 million.

MARSAL: We were able to finance and afford literally getting next to nothing for the hospital we shut down. It turns out to be worth less than $5 million. That's the power of the economics, but for some reason, though in the healthcare industry, you have to convince people that it makes sense. The hard part here was one administration had to go. I think that's the obstacle: it's 50% chance that they'd say that you're going to be the one to go. A lot of hospital administrators are reluctant to consider such a consolidation as that.

ELLISON: Along that line, there is a situation where one of them is a non-profit facility. What are the complications of that situation?

MARSAL: I don't think it's all that difficult in that situation, although I haven't actually done one. However, you have situations where for-profits have purchased the not-for-profit facilities, which sets up the foundation which subsidizes healthcare. Of course, there are a couple of the facilities that have been set up for profit, and there are other situations where a not-for-profit involves a for-profit situation. For example, Mission Viejo is simply a not-for-profit acquisition that may be there for a profit-sharing.

AUDIENCE: With a for-profit or a not-for-profit, there would have to be a repayment of the bond issue, and it would have to be somewhere in that equation of consolidation to take care of that.

MARSAL: Well, I just recently looked at an interesting situation in Texas, where Champion Healthcare has an option to buy a tax-exempt facility, if its method is in hospitals in Jacksonville, if they have guaranteed the tax-exempt bond issue to take the option of five years, and they had their guarantee, of course. They have little choice, but the tax-exempt issue will have to be appeased.

PANELIST: We've faced that situation where we ran out of time trying to find a trustee or a group of investors with whom to negotiate who will sign off on anything. We ran out of time, and filed Chapter 11 in thirty days. It was the bond-holder committee. It was a group of bond-holders who held a representative percentage in the outstanding issue and that's what we negotiated with. We had someone who had authority to sign off on a plan, that was confirmed. If I remember correctly, you were . . . we paused at Chapter 11 for about 160 days.

PANELIST: Nothing happened. Life goes on, nothing changes.

PANELIST: What happens to the boards? How do they feel about them?

PANELIST: I don't know that they may have feelings. There's economic reality. Again, I think that one thing I would echo here is that the name of the game in Chapter 11 is cash flow, not professional liability.

PANELIST: The moral liability is a very, very serious question. I think as we go through the restructuring, particularly with some of the orders, they have their minds set that they are not going to allow resources to dissipate. I'm not sure that they would keep that forever. We sit down, we talk about models, and we talk about forming some of the subsidiaries that are doing statutory mergers one into the other, taking out all of the debt and so forth, so you can say that if it doesn't work out you don't have any personal liabilities. It doesn't matter whether we have separate liabilities or not, we have a moral obligation in our community to stand behind that debt, and/or that mind set may or may not be able to survive. Anyone to comment on this situation?

SPEAKER: Is anybody familiar with any of the non-profits that have been discussed? Yes, Judy.

ELLISON: I have one situation right now with a client, and it's a Chapter 11. It's a non-profit with a Cal Mortgage clause. It's not only a Chapter 11, but three months after the trustee took it over, it closed with about 40 patients. Now the trustee is in a situation where he's building a brand new hospital. They're trying to find a situation where someone will come in. The trustee of the real estate property has been looking at it in terms of real estate solutions.

PANELIST: In the California setting, at least, when you look at a hospital and think of finding alternative uses in doing condominium type approach, or something like that, you run into the elimination of your grandfather clause from the size and safety and other building standards and situation. It is designed at this point to stop you from doing that restructuring, so that the hospital in Los Angeles on Beverly Drive and Pico tries to rescue itself, by going through that and creating different uses. The cost of redoing the building was so astronomical that they were unable to pull it off. They had to close the structure. One last question before we take our break. Anyone? Any comment?

AUDIENCE: I have one question, I'm just curious, because one of the speakers this morning talked about redeploying capital in other healthcare businesses, physician network expansion, home health agencies, and so on. I want to get a comment from the bankers, as to whether they appreciate that as a fundamentally different business from the hospital business and appreciate as well, the amount of the inherent risk that these ventures are, as they get into risk assumption and prepaid managed care, and the capacity really to lose tremendous amounts of monies in those four ways.

MEMEL: The question was for the bankers.

PANELIST: In some cases you have really two ways of proceeding. Number one, and particularly in the non-profit setting, there is little understanding or appreciation of the notion of rates. We try to motivate the notion of really working in the investment area. The second is we know best where the industry is going. Ultimately, the next chapter is going to be hospitals and physicians contracting directly with lawyers to the detriment of some of the managed care plans in many of the markets. Most of the components that the hospital is addressing make sense in that configuration.

PANELIST: There are some fine operations in the industry. I think it is the fact that many people in one segment of the healthcare industry are not very good at running something in every segment of the healthcare business, and that's where sometimes some of the risk is. They don't really know that these businesses are very different.

THE EXPERTS SHOW YOU HOW TO DO IT:

A CASE STUDY

THE EXPERTS SHOW YOU HOW TO DO IT: A CASE STUDY

In this final Part V, we bring together a panel of experts to tackle a hypothetical case study that embodies many, if not all, of the primary challenges facing healthcare organizations today. This is where theory meets practice, and where the reader has a chance to observe how these experts go about solving today's real-world problems. We begin with a detailed presentation of the facts and issues and then move on to identify and choose among the alternative possible solutions.

List of Speakers and Co. Affiliation

Gregory A. Adams
President/CEO
Saint Bernardine Medical Center
San Bernardino, California

George H. Bristol
Director, Corporate Finance
Ernst & Young
Los Angeles, California

Judy Pierson Ellison
President
Quadrant Group, Inc.
Los Angeles, California

Rick L. Grossman, Esq.
Manatt, Phelps & Phillips
Los Angeles, California

Nancy L. Milby
Partner
KPMG Peat Marwick LLP
Long Beach, California

Jeffrey S. Pion
First Vice President
CB Commercial
Los Angeles, California

Eric A. Tuckman, Esq.
Vice President and General Counsel
Centinela Hospital Medical Center
Inglewood, California

HEALTH CARE/REAL ESTATE
SHERATON GRAND - FEBRUARY 9, 1995
A Case Study

MEMEL: We're going to have a group of speakers who will be introduced to you who represent a wide diversity of backgrounds and who will participate in a spontaneous analysis of the situation which is going to be presented to you. We have a hypothetical in your book; what Rick Grossman is going to do is take you through the elements of this case study, and then one of our panelists will take you through an analytical approach quickly to how you might approach a situation like this; and then the panelists will talk about solutions.

Now if somebody in the audience has a strong urge to jump in and say, "why don't you do this or why don't you think of that?" please just indicate that you'd like to ask a question, and the moderator will recognize you. Hopefully by the time this panel finishes with its remarks, you will see the complexity of the problems facing the Boards and the executives in the health care arena all around the country, and particularly in California. You will see why they need real estate solutions, as well as operating solutions to many of their issues, but more importantly, you'll see how they are in almost every way, intertwined and inseparable. I'll call on Ron Barak to make the introductions and get us started.

BARAK: Did Sherwin say that by the time we get through this case study you may have some sense of the complexity that's involved in these matters? My experience is that you probably already have the sense of that complexity. You might not be here if you didn't. What hopefully will come of this next hour is that, in addition to a sense of the complexity, with any bit of luck, you'll also have a sense of the solutions or the alternative possible solutions; and if not altogether the solutions, then at least some sense of disciplined methodology for getting to solutions.

By way of my own experience in real estate workouts in this particular industry, let me offer just a couple of general opening perspectives:

First, as in the real world, you're going to see a very complicated set of facts. We did this by design because that's how the real world works. We could have made the hypothetical easier, but it would have eliminated one of the things that we think is important, viewing a complicated set of facts and figuring out how to separate what is important from what may not be so important. This is critical to effecting the solution process. Keep a couple of other key ingredients in mind from my experience:

Look at the management. Do you have the right kind of management to solve what you need to solve? Capital. Obviously. Do you have the capital? Are you going to need more? Where are you going to get it? How much time do you have to get a solution? Finally, how does this all start to come together into some kind of a cohesive plan?

Again, the resumes are in your materials, and I don't know if they are in the order I have listed here. Now, by way of introduction, we have with us for this case study, Gregory Adams, the Chief Executive Officer of St. Bernadine Medical Center in San Bernardino; George Bristol, the Director of Corporate Finance for Ernst & Young in Los Angeles; Judy Ellison, the president of Quadrant Group L.A.; Rick Grossman, Manatt, Phelps; Nancy Milby, a partner in the health care area, and the taxation field in particular, at KPMG Pete Marwick in Long Beach; Jeffrey Pion, First Vice President of CB Commercial in Los Angeles; and Eric Tuckman, Vice President and General Counsel of Centinela Hospital here in Inglewood.

I thought we would start out with Rick, who gets the credit, for taking the lead on putting this together. You have a text statement in the materials that's probably 15 or 20 pages long. Rick is going to start us off with some slides -- on the theory "a picture's worth a thousand words." Rick.

Rick Grossman
Manatt, Phelps & Phillips
Los Angeles, CA

RICK GROSSMAN: Good afternoon, ladies and gentlemen. I'm a partner at Manatt, Phelps & Phillips with Ron and Sherwin. I work in the health law department. When Ron and Sherwin asked me to put together a case study, I sat down and thought about all the different problems that I've worked on over the last 10 years in the health law field, and I put them all down into 10 pages. For those people that have been able to read the case study that work in the industry, every single one of them has told me that it reflects everything that's happened at their specific institution, although no specific institution has been in mind. Suffice it to say, it's a universal set of facts.

First of all, the case study starts out with a community hospital system, and I've tried to lay out to you an organizational structure. We have the parent organization ABC Health System, Inc., which is defined in the case study as AHS. They're a nonprofit organization and they're tax exempt under Section 501(c)(3). They're the parent organization. They're a subsidiary, nonprofit subsidiary; there's Los Coyotes Medical Center, which is also a nonprofit, and it's also a 501(c)(3) organization. They have a skilled nursing facility, and they have some medical office buildings; basically that's the organizational structure of this particular case.

Here is a little bit of history. As is or was very popular and typical here in Southern California, Los Coyotes started out as a physician hospital (with 99 beds), because in the old days there were some loose regulatory schemes for a 99 bed hospital. They never went over 100. It was built in 1968. The physician-owners added a wing in 1976, and they increased the capacity to 200 beds; then because the debt associated with the increase from 99 to 200 beds was too significant for the physicians, they decided to go nonprofit. This was another scheme that took place in the mid-70's. They formed a new nonprofit corporation and they sold the hospital for $25 million dollars. We'll learn in a moment, where the $25 million dollars came from.

Los Coyotes added a third wing in 1983, to increase their capacity to 300 beds, and that's where they are today. They are located in a suburban neighborhood of L.A. County, and they have some recognized services for which they are fairly well known. For example, they are well known for cardiovascular surgery, cardiology, oncology, obstetrics, and pediatrics. The parent organization was formed in 1982, and as most hospital systems went through the early 80's corporate reorganization, AHS did too. They followed the trend of everybody else.

Now, let's discuss the skilled nursing facility. AHS constructed the skilled nursing facility in 1984, as a three-story 125 bed facility. It's located about 3 miles from the campus of the medical center and after construction was completed, it operated for 3 years at a loss by AHS. Then they ceased the operations. One of the wonderful for-profit side companies came around in 1988 and said, "We want to run an acute psychiatric program, and we'll take your skilled nursing facility." They leased it for 20 years at an annual rent. That is wonderful because AHS was getting money for a facility that they couldn't operate other than at a loss. Thus, the for-profit side management company took up the facility. They reconfigured it as an acute psychiatric facility and started to operate.

And then guess what? In 1993, the rug falls out of the psych industry and the psych company goes into bankruptcy. Simon was talking about bankruptcy before. Many couple-side companies went through bankruptcy. Through that process they negotiated the termination of the lease and gave the property back to AHS. They got a little bit of money in exchange for the remainder of the term of their 20 year lease; clearly not the value of the 20 year lease based upon the substantial annual rent. For the last 2 years, the facility has remained empty because AHS just doesn't know what to do with it.

They also have medical office buildings. They have two of them. They were constructed during the 1980's adjacent to the medical center. When they first opened up the facilities as many hospital did, they offered free rent, below market rent and other incentives to the community physicians, in order to get them to move their offices right next door to the hospital. They quickly leased up the facility, and over a period of years they had a high occupancy of 98%, not atypical for a medical center based MOB.

Until about 18 months ago, when a couple of physicians died, and a couple of physicians retired, their occupancy dropped down to about 80%. Now, after a period of 10 years, most of the rents are at or near market, but there are still a few physicians that have some sweet deals. As is typical with most 1980's MOBs, they're designed for 1 or 2 physician suites and they refinanced it. If you read through the facts a little bit more in detail here, you'll see that in 1989, they refinanced the MOBs for $20 million dollars. And guess what? That amount of debt has a balloon payment which will be due on December 31, 1996. Therefore, as we talk about drop-dead dates, there's an important date for all of us to remember.

The Albatross, the capital debt structure was described earlier. Well, it was mentioned earlier that they originally incurred $25 million dollars in tax exempt debt to acquire the medical center from the physician owners. In 1983, in order to build the skilled nursing facility, expand the medical center, and enlarge the emergency department, they incurred another $30 million dollars of tax exempt debt. Then, in 1988, they decided it was time to refinance; they went out to the market, they refinanced, and they took out another $10 million dollars in order to make some general improvements to their 20 year old facility. Now they have $65 million dollars of tax exempt debt, which they refinanced in 1993, to take advantage of some of the lower interest rates that were available at that time. Their outstanding tax exempt debt is insured by the Cal Mortgage Program.

What else do we need to know about this facility? We've talked about this health system and we've talked about the facilities. Now, let's talk about some other environmental issues: the physician medical staff matters. First of all, the medical staff is typical. It's comprised primarily of well regarded specialists, who built their tertiary care programs. They have a few high quality primary care physicians, but not very many. Most of their physicians are in solo or small single specialty group practices, and the largest medical group on the campus consists of 6 orthopedists. They have an IPA, which they formed in 1986, and it's also controlled by the specialists. An IPA, for those of you who are not actively in the health industry, is an association of independent physicians who come together on a loose association, or contract with HMOs to provide care to HMO enrollees. They formed one in 1986. It currently has about 12,000 covered lives, HMO enrollees that receive care through the IPA and they always operate at a loss; that's principally because they don't have any primary care physicians and the specialists refuse to perform any utilization review. They refuse to control the care that's being provided by themselves, the specialists. What has the health system done? It's underwritten the operating losses which are currently at $3.5 Million Dollars. Again, I think that anyone in hospital operations in this room can appreciate these facts, because they are accurate.

What's their current financial condition? Well, the demographics of the service area have shifted. At one time it was a suburban neighborhood of L.A. County with lots of young people. Today, demographics have changed. They've shifted to Medicare, Medi-Cal, and other people in their community are now enrolled in HMOs and other managed care plans. An example of this phenomenon is that the indemnity insurance payments represented only 8% of net revenues during the last fiscal year, and operating margins have eroded. They have taken typical steps, and have reduced personnel. They also have reduced overhead, and operating expenses. Average daily census has declined, and for the first time the medical center last year operated at a significant loss. The medical center has PPO contracts, and it has per diem contracts with HMOs, but they're still operating at a significant loss.

Now where's the hero? Or one of the heroes? There's Mountain Lion Medical Group. This is typical with many communities; Mountain Lion is a large physician multi-specialty medical group that's located in the community. They have 40 primary care physicians and approximately 35 specialists. They provide services to 95,000 people and about 45,000 are PPO and other types of patients. Most of the physicians have medical staff privileges at the medical center, but they don't regularly use the medical center because of historical issues. Unfortunately, most of you haven't had a chance to read the expository description, but the historical issues are that the founders of Mountain Lion Medical Group weren't allowed to invest in the original hospital when it was built in 1968. For 30 years, they've held a grudge; this is not atypical of what we experienced.

They recently acquired a primary care practice of a physician that's closely affiliated with AHS, and they've approached several other physicians. Their business plan calls for a closer affiliation with a hospital provider, as they look towards full risk computation, and they're looking for clinic sites that's closer to the medical center.

Finally, what's going on recently? What happened yesterday at the medical center at AHS? Well, there are three things that have happened very recently. First of all, AHS has been participating in some discussions with two other small community hospitals similarly situated, operating at front or "break-even", and they're talking about forming a managed care contracting network. In addition, AHS was contacted by Big Pine Hospital System. Big Pine is a for-profit hospital management company that has facilities in 32 States, and they're interested in acquiring the medical center, but they don't want that skilled nursing facility, and those medical office buildings. They're just in the hospital management business.

Big Pine feels that they can purchase the hospital inexpensively, and operate it efficiently. Finally, Mountain Lion Medical Group has approached AHS about leasing the vacant office space in the medical office buildings, in order to raise the possibility about perhaps building a closer working relationship between AHS and the medical group. That is our case, and I know I went through it quickly. You all have it in front of you; both the lengthy version and the outline, and it will be the basis for our discussion.

CASE STUDY
ORGANIZATIONAL STRUCTURE

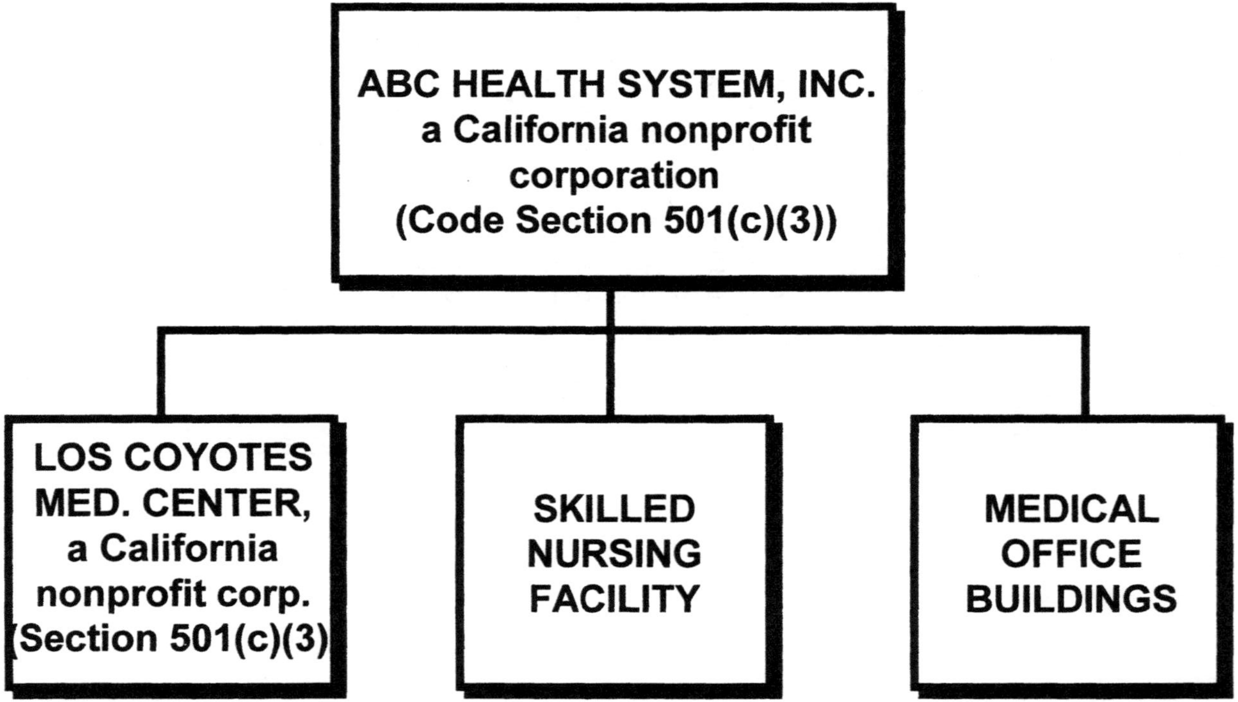

CASE STUDY - HISTORY OF LOS COYOTES MEDICAL CENTER

- PHYSICIANS FOUNDED IN 1968 AS 99 BED COMMUNITY HOSPITAL
- OWNERS ADDED WING IN 1976 AND INCREASED CAPACITY TO 200 BEDS
- OWNERS FORMED NEW NONPROFIT CORPORATION WHICH ACQUIRED HOSPITAL IN 1978 FOR $25 MILLION
- THIRD WING ADDED IN 1983 TO INCREASE CAPACITY TO 300 BEDS
- LOCATED IN SUBURBAN NEIGHBORHOOD OF L. A. COUNTY
- RECOGNIZED AS A REGIONAL TERTIARY CARE FACILITY WITH SIGNIFICANT PROGRAMS IN CARDIOVASCULAR SURGERY, CARDIOLOGY, ONCOLOGY, OBSTETRICS AND PEDIATRICS
- ABC HEALTH SYSTEM, INC (AHS) FORMED IN 1982 AS CORPORATE PARENT ORGANIZATION

CASE STUDY
SKILLED NURSING FACILITY

- CONSTRUCTED IN 1984 AS THREE STORY, 125 BED FACILITY
- LOCATED 3 MILES FROM CAMPUS OF LOS COYOTES MEDICAL CENTER
- OPERATED BY AHS FOR 3 YEARS AT A LOSS BEFORE CEASING OPERATIONS
- LEASED TO FOR-PROFIT PSYCHIATRIC MANAGEMENT COMPANY IN 1988 FOR 20 YEARS AT SUBSTANTIAL ANNUAL RENT
- FOR-PROFIT PSYCHIATRIC MANAGEMENT FACILITY RECONFIGURED FACILITY TO OPERATE AS AN ACUTE PSYCHIATRIC FACILITY
- FOR-PROFIT PSYCHIATRIC COMPANY FILED FOR CHAPTER 11 PROCEEDING IN 1993 AND NEGOTIATED A TERMINATION OF THE LEASE IN EXCHANGE FOR A MONETARY SETTLEMENT PAYMENT
- FACILITY IS CURRENTLY EMPTY

CASE STUDY
MEDICAL OFFICE BUILDINGS

- 2 OFFICE TOWERS CONSTRUCTED DURING 1980s ADJACENT TO MEDICAL CENTER
- FREE RENT, BELOW-MARKET RENT AND OTHER INCENTIVES OFFERED BY AHS RESULTED IN QUICK LEASING OF FACILITY
- OPERATING AT 98% OF CAPACITY UNTIL 18 MONTHS AGO WHEN OCCUPANCY DROPPED TO 80%
- CURRENT RENTAL RATES AT OR NEAR MARKET WITH LIMITED EXCEPTIONS
- MOST OFFICE SUITES ARE DESIGNED AS ONE OR TWO PHYSICIAN SUITES
- REFINANCED IN 1989 FOR $20 MILLION WHICH HAS A BALLOON PAYMENT DUE ON 12/31/96

CASE STUDY
AHS CAPITAL DEBT STRUCTURE

- $25 MILLION OF TAX EXEMPT DEBT INCURRED IN 1978 TO ACQUIRE MEDICAL CENTER
- $30 MILLION OF ADDITIONAL TAX EXEMPT DEBT INCURRED IN 1983 TO FUND CONSTRUCTION OF SKILLED NURSING FACILITY, 1983 EXPANSION OF MEDICAL CENTER AND 1983 ENLARGEMENT OF EMERGENCY DEPT.
- IN 1988, REFINANCED EXISTING TAX EXEMPT DEBT ($55 MILLION) AND INCURRED AN ADDITIONAL $10 MILLION OF TAX EXEMPT DEBT FOR GENERAL IMPROVEMENTS TO MEDICAL CENTER
- $65 MILLION OF TAX EXEMPT DEBT REFINANCED IN 1993.
- OUTSTANDING TAX EXEMPT DEBT IS INSURED BY THE CAL MORTGAGE PROGRAM.

CASE STUDY
MEDICAL STAFF/PHYSICIAN MATTERS

- MEDICAL STAFF COMPRISED PRIMARILY OF WELL REGARDED SPECIALISTS WHO BUILT TERTIARY CARE PROGRAMS
- FEW HIGH QUALITY PRIMARY CARE PHYSICIANS
- MOST PHYSICIANS ARE IN SOLO OR SMALL SINGLE SPECIALTY GROUP PRACTICES
- LARGEST MEDICAL GROUP ON CAMPUS IS 6 ORTHOPEDISTS
- IPA FORMED WITH ASSISTANCE OF AHS IN 1986 AND IS CONTROLLED BY SPECIALISTS
- IPA HAS APPROXIMATELY 12,000 COVERED LIVES AND OPERATES AT A LOSS DUE TO LACK OF PRIMARY CARE PHYSICIANS AND POOR U/R
- AHS UNDERWRITES IPA OPERATING LOSSES ($3.5 MILLION)

CASE STUDY
AHS FINANCIAL CONDITION

- DEMOGRAPHICS OF SERVICE AREA HAVE SHIFTED TO MEDICARE, MEDI-CAL AND MANAGED CARE PATIENTS

- INDEMNITY INSURANCE PAYMENTS REPRESENTED ONLY 8% OF NET REVENUES DURING LAST FISCAL YEAR

- OPERATING MARGINS HAVE ERODED OVER SEVERAL FISCAL YEARS AND STEPS TAKEN TO REDUCE PERSONNEL, OVERHEAD AND OPERATING EXPENSES

- AVERAGE DAILY CENSUS HAS RAPIDLY DECLINED OVER SEVERAL FISCAL YEARS

- MEDICAL CENTER OPERATED AT SIGNIFICANT LOSS DURING ITS MOST RECENT FISCAL YEAR

- MEDICAL CENTER HAS MANY PPO CONTRACTS AND "PER DIEM" CONTRACTS WITH MOST HMOs

CASE STUDY
MOUNTAIN LION MEDICAL GROUP

- 75 PHYSICIAN MULTISPECIALTY MEDICAL GROUP LOCATED IN AHS SERVICE AREA
- 40 PRIMARY CARE PHYSICIANS AND 35 SPECIALISTS IN MULTIPLE FIELDS
- 95,000 HMO COVERED LIVES AND 45,000 PPO AND OTHER PATIENTS
- MOST PHYSICIANS HAVE MEDICAL STAFF PRIVILEGES AT MEDICAL CENTER BUT DON'T REGULARLY USE BECAUSE OF HISTORICAL ISSUES
- RECENTLY ACQUIRED A PRIMARY CARE PRACTICE OF A PHYSICIAN CLOSELY AFFILIATED WITH AHS AND APPROACHED SEVERAL OTHER PHYSICIANS AFFILIATED WITH AHS
- BUSINESS PLAN FOR MEDICAL GROUP CALLS FOR CLOSER AFFILIATION WITH A HOSPITAL PROVIDER
- LOOKING FOR CLINIC SITE CLOSER TO MEDICAL CENTER

CASE STUDY
RECENT DEVELOPMENTS

- AHS PARTICIPATING IN DISCUSSIONS WITH 2 SMALL NONPROFIT COMMUNITY HOSPITALS OPERATING AT "BREAK EVEN" ABOUT FORMING A MANAGED CARE CONTRACTING NETWORK

- AHS CONTACTED BY BIG PINE HOSPITAL SYSTEM, A FOR-PROFIT HOSPITAL MANAGEMENT COMPANY WITH FACILITIES IN 32 STATES, ABOUT THE ACQUISITION OF THE MEDICAL CENTER EXCLUDING SKILLED NURSING FACILITY AND OFFICE BUILDINGS

- MOUNTAIN LION MEDICAL GROUP APPROACHED AHS ABOUT LEASING VACANT OFFICE SPACE IN THE OFFICE BUILDINGS AND RAISED POSSIBILITY OF A CLOSER WORKING RELATIONSHIP BETWEEN AHS AND MEDICAL GROUP

MEMEL: All right, now that you've got the facts well under command, we're going to pass out the quiz and see how many of you have the perfect solution in mind. While you're getting ready to fill it out, George Bristol is going to start us down the right path.

BRISTOL: When we get involved in a number of situations like this, the first thing you have to do is get the Board on target. Many times the Boards don't really understand the urgency of the situation. What we try to do is get the Board to understand where the hospital is today, and where it's got to be in the future, to ensure that management gets its act together. As a result, they can go to the Board and get quick response and action. These things occur, and this is the current state of the hospital or the delivery system. You are essentially creating a managed care environment, a managed care network.

You've got to get your costs in line. But we all need the exercise, hopefully, to provide long term viability . . .

MEMEL: George, let me interrupt one second. Can you see this? Is this focused okay out there?

AUDIENCE: No.

BRISTOL: Well, you really don't need to see this. The important thing is that in any of this process, you've got to get the Board involved. That's really the important part. Other things can happen and many hospitals say, in this case, that "it can't get any worse". The reality is that there are a number of things that can happen in any health care environment, and these things can occur unexpectedly.

For example, you can lose a contract, or a contract may go to somebody else new in the environment; or a competing facility gets sold locally and disrupts everything. A large medical group will be sold to someone else and those referral patterns will change; what results are alliances between unlikely partners. The thing to keep in mind is that things can get worse than they are today. The question comes down to, if you're a free-standing hospital, what is out there for you if you merge with somebody, such as a medical group or another hospital chain? Your board has got to deal with all these issues. I recall situations where we didn't have the Board in the process early on, and consequently, we didn't complete the decision making process. Thus, our whole effort has been to keep the Board moving along at the same time management is coming up with solutions.

The Board has to deal with all these in a environment, where you look at the spectrum of ownership from the stand alone, all the way to where you would sell out to that for-profit hospital.

The other thing that I pointed out is that the strategic process probably takes nine months to actually figure out the strategic alternatives. This hospital is a basket case if they're losing money at a fast rate. The reality is, that if they want to do it in an organized approach, they must realize that it's a complex process.

The reason I discussed these things is that it is complex to try and do some sort of affiliation, while you are dealing with tactical issues. If you're enrolled in the strategic issues, the Board has to decide whether this hospital is really capable of standing alone, or whether it's really got to be part of some large network.

MEMEL: All right. Now, we are going to take Rick Grossman's facts, and George Bristol's criteria and admonitions, and turn it over to our experts here. Let's see what the solution is.

PANELIST: Excuse me, I've seen Judy make some notes. Judy, do you have some opening comments?

ELLISON: I was saving those.

PANELIST: The first question I have is, does AHS have a future and if so, what do they need to do? What direction should they be heading in? My view is that their discussions with the other two primaries, the other two small community hospitals are probably not going to lead them, at least financially, in any direction that's going to be of benefit to them.

ELLISON: I would concur. I think that one of the myths perpetuated about hospitals controlling the system, is that the hospital benefits by just affiliating with a couple of others in the community for contracting reasons. The contracts come from the physicians, and the plans, and they need to really focus their time and attention on trying to get their primary care contracting physician base. Where are they going to get their primary care patients? If you are organizing your primary care physicians, you should try to create a joint venture or a stronger alliance with the group that's in the area.

BRISTOL: The analytical model is critical to what this institution needs to do. Anything it does with real estate really needs to be predicated upon how it responds to the market, and how it sees its future. In addition, I think it's more than just a primary care base; the hospital in terms of the evolution of health care and market reform, really needs work through. It doesn't have the resources or the abilities to be a leader or catalyst, in terms of creating a delivered system, which is more than just aligning with primary care physicians; but it is the ability to capture a large population of managed care lives, and to be at risk for those lives, which includes obviously the insurance piece, the physician piece, and it includes geographical disbursement. I think that is key. Can it be a leader?

If it is not able to be a leader, then it has to conclude. The hospital can enter into a relationship that's not just an affiliation or a primary care relationship, but can it enter into a relationship with an integrated delivery system. If it is not able to do that, then I think the realities are that there are a lot of hospitals that are not going to be able to do that. Essentially what it would do with its assets would be based upon really working through the fact that the market does not have a role or place for it as an acute care institution.

MEMEL: What about the possibility of selling out to Big Pine? The for-profit company is knocking on its door. They are stuck with a \$20 Million mortgage on the medical building that will be due, and they've got the skilled nursing facility. What complicates the situation is that they have \$65 Million Dollars in taxes and bonds that cover the skilled nursing facility. Therefore, if you're going to sell the hospital to Big Pine, you've got to pay off the bonds for two reasons: (1) because Big Pine is for-profit, and (2) because you can't split off part of the collateral, which is the nursing home. What are the chances of Big Pine being willing to pay them? Refinance that \$65 million as part of this purchase, bearing in mind that this is a tertiary center as the case study indicates. They've got a lot of services. What other factors do we have to know about Big Pine, for example?

BRISTOL: Sherwin, I would say before you get to that going back to what Judy said, I think the attractiveness of this institution is whether it's Big Pine or anyone else. It certainly would be enhanced by focusing first on its primary care physicians, whether that's strengthening its IPA, or whether that's looking at a relationship with a multi-specialty group that's been proposed. If it is able to create that kind of relationship where it has access to 90,000 lives, then I think whether it's Big Pine or any other organization, it will be able to approach the negotiating table with a great deal of leverage.

PANELIST: Sherwin, it might be interesting to realize that the management of this hospital is not going to survive because if there becomes a Mountain Lion affiliated entity, it's very difficult for traditional hospital managers to take the responsibility of being a decapitated medical group. The reality is that the hospital is the cost center, and at that point you become a physician group, not a hospital group; the skills of the hospital managers are probably not in line for what this organization needs long term. That's why a lot of these deals don't happen, because in a nonprofit setting, the executive ends up walking out of the facility without a job.

ELLISON: Another thing that happens is that when Big Pine comes in, they will look at how the hospital is being managed under the nonprofit models, and they will propose major cuts and changes that usually intimidate bright, nonprofit Boards. It is important to protect our service to the community and our quality. A for-profit hospital chain can buy an organization, but one of the first things they're going to do other than looking at where they can get the physicians, is cut operations to the standards that they have, and that might be very unhouseable to the Board. You're right, that administration probably may not be the one to do it.

The one advantage that they have by becoming a part of an integrated system, is that they can begin to effect some operational savings that they might not be able to do when they are on their own. Still that may not get enough to the bottom line to enable them to make it.

One of the issues that you have here is an assumption; you don't know how big this system's war chest is. You have to assume either that they have enough money to weather the storm for some period of time or that they absolutely have no money. It is unlikely in this case that Big Pine with the parameters that were set out, is going to be prepared to pay $65 million or perhaps $50 million dollars. One of the things we don't know is whether the system has enough money to pay off the tax exempt bonds.

As attractive as may be, it may not be possible, because the dollars may not be there. Then you've got a system left with an empty skilled nursing facility, and a medical office building. Again, you don't know whether $20 million dollars will cover their debt service in the medical office building or not. You have to make assumptions about that.

MEMEL: We have a couple of hands up in the audience. Let me respond to the one back there first. You sir. Yes.

QUESTION: The problem is, you really have two timing questions. First, you have an immediate question with the debt being due in '96. Then you have a long term cash flow problem, which is whether we can YTA or MSO, or whatever the terms of the contract dispositions. I think whether you like it or not, you have to deal with Big Pine. You're going to have to resolve the debt problem, which is due immediately. Regarding the two dog pieces of real estate, perhaps you could enter into some sort of a ground piece with Big Pine with a cancellation, or put an option back on the dogs if those two pieces of real estate don't perform in 5 or 7 years; thereby giving you an opportunity to see if you can get your long term cash flow moving along with your IPA scenario. I think somehow you have to integrate both the short-term and a long-term. Put them together. I don't think you can do one or the other.

MEMEL: Simon?

ARON: Do we know if this is at the point where this group is balance sheet insolvent or not? Does this mean their liabilities exceed their assets?

GROSSMAN: No we don't. We know they have $65 Million Dollars of debt and they have ________________ real estate...

PANELIST: Plus operating losses.

PANELIST: Right. So the likelihood is that they're probably from a balance sheet standpoint either at or near --

ARON: Eric's comment is first of the considerations that have to be taken into account. Situations that involve getting boards, and getting decision makers to act may be the biggest hurdles that you have. The Board of Directors and officers of an insolvent enterprise have a fiduciary duty to the creditors, not necessarily to the shareholders and those people; but now the creditors may put that Board on notice, warning that they may need to look beyond its own self interests or self interest of self-preservation to a different scenario, one that includes maximizing value, and things of that nature.

MEMEL: Simon, you can create several scenarios here: (1) this is a parent that was formed by the hospital in order to meet certain regulatory requirements, and to build medical office buildings owned by the parent without certificates of need, instead of having to buy it under the hospital when they had certificate of need in this State. It was formed by the hospital. You can assume that either it has no substantial capital in the parent at all, or you can assume that maybe they've accumulated some capital over the years up there; five, ten, fifteen million dollars, as we find some of our clients saving for a rainy day. With five, ten, or fifteen million dollars, you have to ask yourself if you're trying to do something with a medical group like Mountain Lion, which will not go very far if you're trying to lock those doctors into an affiliation with you, because they're going to want to be bought out. This is happening in big medical group buyouts and that money won't go very far at all.

So you're going to have to figure out a way to get them to align with you. According to the facts in this case, most of their clinics are not located in the immediate proximity of the hospital; they are moving. They're in the service area, but they're moving into your neighborhood. Therefore, we don't know where their other allegiances are, and where they're putting their patients from the other clinics. These are all the real world analyses that you have to go through in this kind of a transaction. In terms of the medical office building, it's separately financed. In the worst case scenario, you can either refinance that debt if you're lucky, or if not, you've got a Chapter 11. Otherwise, you must let them take the building back.

ARON: Handing them the keys may be practical in many situations, but when you have a building that's on the hospital campus, and it is still filled with the physicians that are providing the services for your institution, simply giving the facility back to the bank doesn't always work from a practical standpoint. I would suggest that the issues become significantly more complex because there not only are legal or operational issues, but there are moral issues that override every decision that's made. I'd like to make one comment, and that is that I think the debt which is due in December 31, 1996, provides an opportunity for the institution that's twofold. First, they know they have a target date that they have to meet, and that gives the Board of Directors an opportunity not only to talk to Big Pines, but perhaps to follow George's analysis; that is to go through a strategic process and look at what all their alternatives may be. Their best alternative may not necessarily be Big Pines, it may be the other large nonprofit institution that's looking for a facility in their area that may be willing to extend the process longer than Big Pines. Moreover, they have a period of time to start talking with Mountain Lion, so that when they go to Big Pines or another organization, they can at least represent that they've started the process in discussions with the large medical group. Then, finally they have some period of time to turn their operations around, so that when they have to go back to the bank and either renegotiate their balloon or look for new financing, they may be able to develop some cash flow.

I think the process that George outlined is a very valuable process because by Big Pines stepping forward, this does not mean there is not 2, 3, 5 or other players in the market place that would be interested in talking to this particular institution.

PANELIST: No matter what you do, at least experience in this market place has been that unless you integrate Mountain Lion into this facility, either on an equity basis or long term contract, the relationship is really a nonsolution. This is true because three years from now they'll be knocking at your door saying they got a better deal down the street, and they will be moving their 95,000 lives. Then you will really be out of luck because you have no strategic ability to plan at all. You've got 90 days or 60 days to basically make up for 90,000 captured lives, which is almost impossible in this marketplace.

PANELIST: In terms of the strategic planning process, and in terms of Mountain Lion, I think the other option that would have an impact, both short term and long term, would be to look at transitioning the hospital to the group. This creates a level of integration and access to capital, both short and long term, which the hospital presently does not have. Again, this makes the hospital much more beneficial and attractive to the system in terms of a broader affiliation.

ELLISON: Unfortunately, I have a lot of clients that are in this situation, but, they had two major groups that were loyal one day, and unloyal the next day. They knew that particularly with a Medicare base, that their primary care physicians had a great deal of loyalty from the local community, and they concentrated on organizing their own loyal primary care physicians into a primary care group. Then that group was the leverage to basically tie the other major IPA group to the hospital, because that is the only way Mountain Lion could get market share in that area. Those primary care physicians were able to not only bring those regional contracts, but they were also able to negotiate the use of the hospital's home health car agency, and the use of the hospital's services, so that they worked through them. The other thing I think which nobody's mentioned, is that a skilled nursing facility might not have not been the business for them 10 years ago. It could certainly be a business for them now, and there's so many that they could take all three floors, and lease out those floors to nursing homes, to a sub-acute, you name it. I would start looking for somebody to lease and open up that building.

MEMEL: What I was just going to ask was what Judy just discussed; the alternative uses for the skilled nursing facility or the medical office building. As a lawyer, I have to spoil that by saying that the minute you do that, you jeopardize the tax exempt status of the bonds when dealing with any for profit agencies.

ELLISON: But there are lots of nonprofits out there.

MEMEL: It is going to narrow your market down. You're going to have to find someone in the nonprofit field, who would be willing to make use of that building. If there is good use of that building, then why don't *you* do it? Is it because the capital is too high? Those are some of the questions you have to ask yourself.

ELLISON: I would suggest to Sherwin two things. First of all, that the for-profit service management companies, whether they be rehab companies, skilled nursing, subacute care and all the other types of health organizations, are now entering hospitals to manage various types of services. They could easily work out a management arrangement, which would not cause their tax exempt bonds to lose their tax exempt status, but put the management company in a position of putting up some of the capital, in order to retrofit or improve a facility for a new service. Then they could enter into a long term or a longer term arrangement with the hospital for the management of that service, and both entities can profit from that. That may be a step over the next two years to 18 months that the facility should be looking at. We've mentioned skilled nursing. I think that again the facts don't really talk about outpatient services that the medical center is involved with. It may be that they could take one of the floors, and actually turn that into an outpatient department, and use that for some services, whether it's an outpatient surgery center or some other types of out patient services. Then allow the other floors to be managed as sub-acute care, skilled nursing, etc.

ELLISON: If you remember the slide that Judy showed you on the continuum of care, I think that if you stop thinking of the real estate as a problem for a minute, and look at it as an opportunity, you can build almost all of the components of that continuum of care within the real estate facilities that you have right there in front of you. It's going to take the cooperation of bringing in a Mountain Lion or other big medical group to make that happen. Even though the two year date for the balloon payment is something that should give you the impetus to move, it shouldn't be the focus point in terms of trying to solve that problem. It should be the opportunity to solve some of the other bigger problems that you have.

PANELIST: When you first look at the case study, the first responses as somebody in the audience said, there are two dogs; these are the medical office building, and the skilled nursing facility. When you built the nursing facility in '84 it operated at a loss for 3 years before they closed it. Well, now as everybody's saying it's an asset, and a chance to be part of the continuum. You still have a problem with the medical office building because you've got 18 months to do something with that. You either have to sell it, or refinance it, which will cost you capital. If you make the assumption that because they refinanced it in '89 for $20 million at least in California it's probably under water, and there's very little equity and refinance, and some type of a workout is going to cost you money in capital. The question is, whether that capital is best used for the real estate, to do a transaction with Mountain Lion, or to be part of an integrated delivery system.

MEMEL: Mike?

STEPHENS: There are a couple of other complication that come to mind. I know this is exhilarating.

MEMEL: . . . and it has a seismic problem.

ELLISON: It's one of your bread and butter clients Michael?

STEPHENS: We all know this facility because it was built 15 times, 18 times or something over 1968 '69 and it's a one story facility; it's a cookie cutter, it's replicated, it has the entire facility with all of the components. It's been expanded over a period of time and the oldest part of that hospital has been wrapped around by the two or three operating rooms that have been added onto the radiology group. The beds have been wrapped around the core of this building in 1968, the building being the center of the entire campus. We're looking at this short term of 2 years to 6 years. Add to this the state seismic model. That's going to add some capital requirements over a period of time. Any time you try to upgrade, it will trigger major increases in dollars. So, you really have to look at the long range or you try to do short term solutions in the long range. Part of that facility can be replaced and rebuilt over a time. Picture that organization over 5 years, or 10 years. Are the facilities really an albatross?

MEMEL: But other than that it's all right?

PANELIST: I think the focus here is to get the attention of the Board, and ask them why they got involved with the hospital initially. Then realize that function or that purpose is no longer there. The institution is no longer the center of the delivery system, and they would be comfortable with being a member of a Board of a foundation that provides other services in the community, that are akin to why they got on the Board initially. As you talk to the Board members more and more, they realize the difficulties of running this large expense-eating-institution, and they realize that there really is no future. They realize more and more that they can add more to the community by perhaps being part of a foundation, and that maybe it is time to wrap it up, close, and work out some sort of deal with the bondholders. The reality is that this particular institution is probably not going to support this debt for much longer.

PANELIST: My observation would be that it takes at least 3 months to get them to move along, they're going to be business people, and they're eventually going to say, "You can't tell me that my choices are to write this debt down by 50% or 60%. There's gotta be another choice." You must get the Board to buy early on. You must go through some sort of ration process to prove to them what the value is. If it is a major upside down capitalization, you must file Chapter 11. You have to do it sooner or later. The whole process really from a management point of view, is to get the Board to understand what the process is, and to report back to them quickly, so you don't let this thing run on for a year or two. This could really reduce your assets. Someone stated earlier that the value of hospitals will not increase; that the value will slowly erode in time. Therefore, you start the process now if it's not going to be the lead player in a managed care network . . . .

PANELIST: One other option that we've talked about is that there may come a time where the plan is to decide that they want to stop operating as institutional providers. There might be an option of going to Big Pine or one of these large plans, and deciding that now is the time to cut out the profit on the hospital side, and buy us out. I think there's a possibility for some of the large HMOs across the country to perhaps return to the institutional side of it.

MEMEL: All right so let me, Greg, go ahead and then I'll...

ADAMS: I'm one of those people that's not in this hospital today, but could be tomorrow. I think the realities are that there are too many hospitals, and if the group has 90,000 lives it's working with at least 2 or 3 other hospitals in this particular area. It would be ideal if you could sit down with the Board, and in three months get them to agree to close or to do something different; that's probably not going to happen. I would expect that in today's current environment, what will probably happen involves refinancing, or working some limited relationship with the group. There are many of them out there, we live with them daily, and it will struggle. It will continue to struggle. It will probably go through a lot of out patient programs, and different services, which still won't service the debt until the market reaches a point, where we will begin to look at these facilities clearly as what we do with them; it won't be health care. It will be a question of whether we level them, or come up with other uses.

MEMEL: Psychiatric jail facilities.

ADAMS: I think that we're going to get there in the next 3-5 years.

MEMEL: All right. Let's take a couple minutes here to see if we can recap somewhat and make some decisions. We'll be a hypothetical Board of Directors in this room. This group is a little too large, but it will suffice.

PANELIST: I have clients this big.

MEMEL: I have clients this big, but not boards this big.

PANELIST: I mean I have clients with boards this big.

MEMEL: I could think of one, but they don't have these problems.

To recap a little bit, I made a listing of the comments here, and I came up with 5 points. We have to deal with the Board. For a moment, you are not the Board. You will be, though. The Board has the natural human egos and its problems. It has had a healthy history, and now it's finding itself tired and with a lot of challenges. We maybe have some demographic research to do, because as Judy said, we've got that SNF that is sitting there doing nothing. This whole campus has got to have some more life built back into it, and it needs more doctors of one kind or another. It needs some kind of revenue to give to that skilled nursing facility that is empty. It has an office building that has been carrying itself, but as Jeff says, it's clearly got a negative value. There's no equity in that building right now, based on when it was refinanced, based on the hypothetical facts of its occupancy. There's no way in today's market that you refinance that as it is right now; you have to infuse capital. This means you have to rely on Mountain Lion to bring in more doctors. You must also get Big Pine to bring some life there. If not Big Pine, maybe you have to shop against some of the competitors of Big Pine. If you find an alternative use, there is the option of preserving our tax exempt obligations and financing by using some kind of a ground lease mechanism, in order to keep the ownership and your tax exempt financing in place. You can ground lease it out to someone who's going to put it to a use that your demographic study tells you will work, and have a place in the market. Now we are the Board of Directors. What's the plan? Are we talking about liquidating? Are we talking about a type of orderly liquidation? Or, do we really think that there is something here with these variables that's worth pursuing and can lead to a solution? You can't be wishful thinkers here. You have to make the hard decision. We are going to take a little survey. You have to make the hard decision for the moral obligations. You're only a year or two away until that $20 Million debt is due on that office building. There is no way that you can refinance it, and there's no way that a Chapter 11 bankruptcy proceeding is going to help you. It might stall it for a few months, but that lender is going to get relief because you have no equity, and no plan as yet that has crystallized. So let's just get some wrap-up comments here of you on the Board of Directors. What do you think? Here, and here.

PANELIST: I think one of the first things that you have to do to address virgin problems is to go to Mountain Lion and try to cut a deal with them, to open up a clinic in my medical office building because that helps me with cash flow. Integrate the skilled nursing facility. Then you have to look at the big picture issues, which I'm going to let my colleagues deal with.

PANELIST: Well, I would be bold enough I think, as long as it's not me next year, to address the skilled nursing facility issue. That's certainly one that can be addressed. I think that I probably would encourage the physician group not to solely look at leasing space. I think this is a facility that probably needs to transition, and to truly integrate the system, the group needs a large out patient base. The idea is to take over, and operate and integrate this facility.

ELLISON: An alternative would be to look at another large regional medical group that wants to get into that area. Another immediate cash flow opportunity, would be to bring in a MediCal PCCM group: a medical group that provides services to MediCal patients or some group that's headed towards MediCal managed care. Capture that market. And I've seen hospitals . . .

MEMEL: Make sure you keep your answer yes and no when you can, and stick to the question that is asked. You are now the Board. You now have to vote. You know, these things don't come about overnight. It takes time to develop and implement a solution. Is there a solution here worth pursuing, or is this a company to be liquidated?

PANELIST: I think one of things we have to look at is, you have 90,000 HMO lives. Isn't that $1,000.00 per employee in California? Perhaps, it's $1,200. There's $100,000,000 of cash flow right there. It seems to me that the strategy is paying cash out of the other hospitals. He's got $100,000,000 of revenue that you control, and there was a PPO of $20,000 to $30,000. You have the revenues to survive. The question is, do you have the proper ownership? With $100,000,000 or $125,000,000 in tactual revenues, you know, 6.5 or $7,000,000 debt service is not an insignificant __ it's not out of line.

MEMEL: Not insurmountable.

ELLISON: The hospital doesn't have that. The medical group has that.

MEMEL: Any other votes?

PANELIST: The issue is not, you know, whether you have any equity. It's a question of ownership structure. By integrating to two, and by putting the doctors on top of the hospital's cost center, I mean you turn, the sow's ear back into a purse.

PANELIST: The reality of this hypothetical is that the real money to be made currently is on the hospital capitation side, because the medical groups have done a wonderful job on the physician side.

BARAK: That's right.

PANELIST: And the real irony of this from an institutional point of view is that we've gone full circle. This is going to become a physician's hospital again.

BARAK: Yes.

PANELIST: And that's where the industry's going. That's the irony of what's happening.

BARAK: Mr. Cooper, any other up and down votes now? Up and down, up or down, which is it?

COOPER: The answer is yes, Ron. You and I were talking about this at the lunch break; and that is that what I voted for; that has brought your bond trustee and your lenders to the negotiation table. In the numerous workouts I've done, 95% of the time I advise my clients, if you want to negotiate with your lender, stop paying. They play the waiting game. As long as you pay a lender, they're not going to talk to you. Therefore, the first thing you do is default your bonds, and default your loans. That gets them to the table; now you are dealing with all the players and you can put them together in court. Then you'll have your answer shortly, whether you get to deal or call it quits.

BARAK: Simon?

ARON: Yeah, I was going to say that I agree with Dan and the gentlemen behind me. I'm not sure if he took a default or whether he's trying to open that dialogue with a lender, particularly with your bondholders and Cal Mortgage, who are going to be getting an education as to how to deal with these situations. They're starting now and they'll . . . . There is a question of whether you are going to be the teacher or the pupil. I figure in this regard it's going to be people in this industry who are going to be teaching, and not necessarily learning; they are learning now.

BARAK: Right. Aaron?

LATT: I was just going to say that there's a possible equation that's missing. We're talking about facilities that we built years ago. We're talking about selling portions or bringing in other operations, including massive retrofit costs involved with this; and without understanding what those costs are bringing to these facilities up to current ABA and various other requirements. This is a big ingredient. You can't just say, I'll lease this, I'll do this, and I'll do that. Michael touched the subject there. This was built years ago. It may be totally worthless by the time you analyze what all those costs are going to be.

BARAK: Okay, let's do this. We're reaching the "drinking hour." I'll take my moderator's prerogative. I usually like voting in the minority. This time I find myself coming out with the majority, if the physical aspects here that Arron and Michael have mentioned, are not insurmountable. If they're not, financial issues are potentially solvable. You're probably going to have to make some changes in management to pull this off, and to work it all out, but there are the elements here to make this work. I agree with Mr. Cooper, in part, but maybe as Simon refines it a bit. I don't think I'd rush off to default now, but I definitely perceive a default as a positive vehicle. I think there's some more homework to be done in this hypothetical before it's time to do that. I don't mean to suggest that Mr. Cooper wouldn't agree with that. Default and what you get done with your tax-exempt bondholder series, is clearly a major part of this decision.

Since we are at that bewitching hour, I'd just like to make a couple concluding remarks from Sherwin's and my point of view; I'll then let Sherwin speak for himself.

This has been a very interesting experience for us. This is the first annual institute. We hope that there will be interest and reason to do the second annual institute. The healthcare industry, to my observation from a real estate outsider's perspective, is clearly facing challenging times. There's a lot of talent in the healthcare industry and healthcare, like food and housing, is not going to go away. I don't think there's any reason to panic. I think what's basically needed are creative, prompt, and forceful responses; recognition of problems when they're there, rather than trying to pretend they're not there, rather than watching your reserves going down until it's too late to do anything. If people will meet the issues head-on, we're in a very positive business industry. People need the service and the need is growing.

I would like to conclude by thanking a number of people: to all of you for coming, and the University of Southern California for joining our firm to put this together; the advisory committee that you haven't seen today, but which gave us a great deal of help; Ed Poll and his staff, which has done a tremendous job of organizing all of the things that nobody wants to attend to; all of our speakers -- those you see up here now, and those who have been up here earlier today; and last but not least, much thanks to my partner Sherwin Memel. Thank you all very much.

SPEAKERS' RESUMES

SANDRA R. SMOLEY, Secretary, California Health & Welfare Agency

Sandra R. Smoley was appointed as Secretary of the Health and Welfare Agency by Governor Pete Wilson in October of 1993. Smoley is a member of the Governor's Cabinet and serves as his chief advisor on health and social service policy. She manages an agency which employs more than 42,000 employees and has a budget of $36 billion. Previously, Smoley served ass Secretary of the State and Consumer Services Agency where she managed an agency with 15,000 employees and a budget of almost $700 million. Smoley, a registered nurse, received her degree in nursing from the University of Iowa and is a graduate of the Senior Executive Training Program for State and Local Government at Harvard's John F. Kennedy School of Government.

RONALD S. BARAK

Mr. Barak is a partner in the Los Angeles office of Manatt, Phelps & Phillips. He is Chairman of the law firm's Real Estate Department and specializes in leasing, development, joint ventures and finance. Mr. Barak is particularly active in international matters. Mr. Barak began his law practice in the Los Angeles office of Paul, Hastings, Janofsky & Walker. He became a partner in that firm and served as an elected member of that firm's Management Committee and Partner Compensation Committee and as appointed Chairman of that firm's real estate department. Mr. Barak was born in Los Angeles in 1943. In 1964 he graduated with honors from the University of Southern California with a B.S. degree in Physics and was the recipient of the Jacob Gimbel Scholar/Athlete of the Year. In 1968 he graduated from the University of Southern California Law Center with a J.D. degree. In the upper 5% of his class, Mr. Barak served as Associate Editor of the University of Southern California Law Review (based upon class standing and law review performance). He was admitted to the California Bar in 1968 and is also a licensed real estate broker. Mr. Barak speaks and writes frequently on real estate matters. He is the author of *Foreign Investment in U.S. Real Estate*, published in English hardback by Harcourt Brace Jovanovich in 1981 and in Japanese hardback by Press Aid Center, Inc. in 1983. Portions of this book were republished in German hardback as part of *Immobilienanlagen in den USA* by Kristall bei Langen-Muller in 1982. Mr. Barak is also the author of several chapters in *The Commercial Real Estate Tenant's Handbook*, published in English hardback by John Wiley & Sons in 1987, and *Commercial Tenant's Leasing Transactions Guide*, published in English hardback by John Wiley & Sons in 1991. Raised in Los Angeles, where he contines to reside, Mr. Barak is married and has two children. His interests include golf, tennis, Japanese language, computer technology and applications, music, sports, reading and bridge. Mr. Barak has sat as a Judge *Pro Tem* on the Los Angeles Municipal Court, participated in various community and civic activities and was acompeting member of the 1964 U.S. Olympic Team.

SHERWIN L. MEMEL

Sherwin L. Memel is a Senior Partner in the 165-attorney firm of Manatt, Phelps & Phillips, with offices in Los Angeles, Nashville and Washington, D.C. He is Chairman of the Health Law Department, working in virtually every facet of the healthcare industry. Mr. Memel was a founding member and past president of the California Society for Healthcare Attorneys and a founding member of the American Academy of Hospital Attorneys. Mr. Memel also is a former member of the California Board of Medical Quality Assurance, the state licensing entity for physicians and other health personnel and was the Board's first non-physician president. He served as a member of the Federal Health Insurance Benefits Advisory Counsel, the advisory body to Congress and the Social Security Administration on establishment and administration of the Medicare and Medicaid program. Mr. Memel has served as a consultant to major industrial corporations on health business matters and as a university adjunct professor in the health care field. He received both his B.A. and J.D. degrees from the University of California, Los Angeles.

DANIEL M. CAIN

Daniel M. Cain is a founding partner in 1982 and Principal of Cain Brothers, and a widely recognized expert in healthcare finance. He was Senior Vice President of Blyth Eastman Dillon Health Care Funding, Inc.; Vice President and Manager of the Health Care Finance Group at Solomon Brothers. Previously, he worked in corporate and real estate finance at Merrill Lynch. Cain received his B.A. degree from Brown University and an M.B.A. degree in Finance from Columbia University.

MICHAEL J. CALHOUN

Michael J. Calhoun is Vice President of Lewin-VHI, Inc. Previously, he was Hayase Research Fellow at the Asia/Pacific Research Center Stanford University and Visiting Research Fellow at the International Research Center for Japanese Studies. He was Chief of Staff for the U.S. Department of Health and Human Services. Mr. Calhoun was a partner in Finley, Kumble, Wagner, Heine, Underberg, Manley, Myerson and Casey and previously served as Assistant Minority Counsel for International Trade on the Committee on Ways and Means, U.S. House of Representatives. Mr. Calhoun received a B.A. from Woodrow Wilson School of Public and International Affairs, Princeton University and a J.D. from Harvard Law School.

MICHAEL D. STEPHENS

Michael D. Stephens is the President of Hoag Memorial Hospital Presbyterian, a 416 bed not-for-profit facility with a $315 million revenue budget. Mr. Stephens is a member of the Board of Directors of Blue Cross of California. He received his B.A. from Columbia College, an M.B.A. from Columbia University and an M.S. in Hospital Administration from Columbia University School of Public Health and Administrative Medicine.

DR. R. TARANTELLO, CRE

Dr. Rocky Tarantello joined the faculty of the University of Southern California in 1974. He currently holds the position of Clinical Associate Professor of Real Estate and Land Economics. He received his Doctor of Business Administration and M.B.A. degrees from the University of Southern California and a B.S. in Business Administration from California State University at Los Angeles. He has extensive experience in real estate development, investment, market research, appraisal and counseling throughout the United States. He is an active member of an Orange County, CA hospital advisory board and a member of the board of directors of the non-profit Southern California Housing Development Corporation. He is president of Tarantello & Associates, a California based real estate counseling company.

MICHAEL BOBROW, AIA

Michael Bobrow is founder and Principal-for-Design of Bobrow/Thomas and Associates, the Los Angeles based architecture, planning and consulting firm. He practices in the field of large scale healthcare architecture and urban design. He founded and directs the Health Facility Design Program at UCLA Graduate School of Architecture and Urban Design and the School of Public Health, one of two such programs in the nation. Mr. Bobrow is a graduate of Columbia University School of Architecture. Before founding BTA in 1972, Mr. Bobrow was Senior Architect in the office of the Air Force Surgeon General.

JUDY PIERSON ELLISON

Judy Pierson Ellison is president of The Quadrant Group. She provides planning services to health care and service organizations. Her focus is the development of innovative and effective health care delivery responses tot he changes in the industry. Previously, Ms. Ellison was a senior principal in the national firm of Laventhol & Horwath where she directed the Los Angeles Health Advisory Services group. She directed an HEW study at LAC-USSC Medical Center on ambulatory care case management and has taught in the Graduate School of Nursing at UCLA. She also was a principal of BTA, Inc in 1972. She received here M.S. in Nursing, University of California, Los Angeles and a B.S. from San Jose State University.

CHARLES H. HARRISON

Charles H. Harrison is a certified public accountant and Partner in Charge of the Southern California healthcare practice of Arthur Andersen & Co. Mr. Harrison has extensive experience in audits and departmental, operational and internal control reviews. He is the firm-wide expert on Home Health Agencies. He received an M.B.A. in Finance and B.S. in Accounting from the University of Southern California.

MARC S. MARGULIS

Marc S. Margulis is Co-Director of the Health Care Practice and a Managing Director in the Los Angeles Office of Houlihan Lokey Howard & Zukin. Mr. Margulis values primary through tertiary healthcare enterprises for M&A, litigation and tax purposes. In addition, he has testified as an expert in economic damages, dissenting shareholder rights, solvency, and in the valuation of intangible assets. Mr. Margulis earned his Bachelor's degree in Political Science and Economics at the University of California, Santa Barbara and an M.B.A. at the University of California, Los Angeles. Mr. Margulis is an Accredited Senior Appraiser and a Charter Financial Analyst.

SIMON ARON

Simon Aron is a partner and head of the Bankruptcy and Creditors' Rights Department of the law firm of Manatt, Phelps and Phillips. His practice involves all aspects of bankruptcy and creditor-debtor rights with particular emphasis on commercial transactions, workouts and reorganizations. Mr. Aron has appeared in numerous bankruptcy cases and related proceedings throughout the United States. Mr. Aron received his B.A. from University of California, Los Angeles and J.D. from Southwestern University School of Law.

BRYAN P. MARSAL

Bryan P. Marsal is a Founding Managing Director of Alvarez & Marsal, Inc. ("A&M"), a firm that was formed in 1983 to provide financial and operational services to troubled companies. Mr. Marsal has led numerous A&M engagements with clients in the healthcare, manufacturing and retailing industries. In this capacity, he has served in numerous chief executive positions including Republic Health Corporation (currently known as ORNDA). In addition, Mr. Marsal has served on the Boards of Directors of Republic Health Corporation, Cherokee Inc., Timex Corporation and The Gladney Center. Prior to A&M, Mr. Marsal was Director of Operations Control of Norton Simon, Inc., where he oversaw the operations planning, analysis and review of four Norton Simon subsidiaries. Prior to joining Norton Simon in 1982, he was a Vice President in the problem loan division of Citibank, N.A. At Citibank, Mr. Marsal managed a workout team and was directly involved in a number of large problem loan situations. Mr. Marsal received both a B.B.A. and an M.B.A. from the University of Michigan.

CRAIG L. McKNIGHT

Craig L. McKnight, a certified public accountant, recently transferred to Philadelphia. While in Los Angeles, he was Partner-in-Charge of the Los Angeles Office Service Industry practice group which includes health care practices. This practice group is responsible for a wide range of clients including major providers of health coverage. He was also responsible for the Health Care practice of the firm on the West Coast. In addition to audit and tax services, Mr. McKnight works with clients in formulating financing options, debt restructuring, credit agreement restructure and the purchase/sale of health plans and facilities.

CHARLES G. PLIMPTON

Charles G. Plimpton is Vice President in the Investment Banking Division and member of the Nuveen Health Care Group. Mr. Plimpton specializes in hospital-related investment banking services. His responsibilities currently encompass financing and advisory services to major health care organizations. Since 1990, Mr. Plimpton has served as the lead banker for 22 health care bond issues totaling over $1 billion in par value. Prior to joining John Nuveen & Co. Incorporated, Mr. Plimpton was an officer of Paine Webber Health Care Funding, Inc. and was associated with the corporate finance division of The Northern Trust Company in Chicago, Illinois. His activities included the arrangement of taxable and tax-exempt corporate related financings and of mergers and acquisitions. Mr. Plimpton received a B.A. from the University of Pennsylvania and an M.B.A. from the Amos Tuck School of Business Administration, Dartmouth College.

ALBERT E. SMITH

Albert E. Smith is Senior Banker of Citibank, N.A., Dallas, TX. He is responsible for a Healthcare origination team. His activities include senior bank debt syndication, M&A advisory, high-yield bond origination, derivatives, securitization and cash management services. He built the bank's Southwest and Western Healthcare asset portfolios. Mr. Smith received a B.A. in English Literature from Westminster College in Missouri and an M.B.A. from the Wharton School of Business, University of Pennsylvania.

GEORGE H. BRISTOL

George H. Bristol is a Partner and the Director of Ernst & Young's West Region Corporate Finance Department located in Los Angeles. He is the Corporate Finance liaison with the firm's Health Care practice. Mr. Bristol has provided financial advisory services to for profit and not for profit health care companies involved in mergers, acquisitions, public and private offerings of debt and equity placements, private placements, reorganizations and debt restructurings. Prior to joining Ernst & Young, Mr. Bristol was a Managing Director for the Corporate Finance Department of Dean Witter Reynolds in Los Angeles; Managing Director and Regional Manager for Prudential-Bache Capital Funding; and First Vice President in the merger and acquisition group at Blyth Eastman Paine Webber in New York. Mr. Bristol received an M.B.A. degree from Harvard Business School with a concentration in Finance, and a B.A. degree from the University of Michigan with concentrations in Economics and Accounting.

NANCY L. MILBY

Nancy L. Milby is a certified public accountant and Partner in KPMG's Pacific Southwest Health Care and Life Sciences Practice. Ms. Milby specializes in providing tax planning and business consulting to partnerships, S corporations and professional corporations. Ms. Milby has extensive experience in both transactional and operational tax issues relating to the health care industry, particularly with respect to medical groups and physician networks, and currently serves as tax engagement partner on both for-profit and not-for-profit entities. Ms. Milby received a bachelor of science degree from the University of California, Berkeley in accounting.

GREGORY A. ADAMS

Gregory A. Adams has more than 20 years experience in the health care industry. He received a nursing degree in 1974 and later a Bachelors of Arts in Business Studies from Ogelthorpe University in Atlanta, Georgia. In 1983 he received a Masters in Administration from Wichita State University. In addition to serving in numerous nursing administration positions, including a position with the Mayo Clinic, Greg served as Executive Vice President/Chief Operating Officer for Baptist Healthcare System, in Beaumont, Texas. In this position he participated in expanding the system from a single hospital to a five hospital system. Greg joined St. Bernardine Medical Center in 1989 as Associate Administrator/Chief Operating Officer. In 1990 he became President/Chief Executive Officer. He is active in numerous professional and community organizations, including Board Member Healthcare Association Southern California and Board of Directors for California Association of Hospital and Health Systems. He speaks widely on health care related issues and has numerous articles and book contributions to his credit.

RICK L. GROSSMAN

Rick L. Grossman is a Partner in the Health Law Group of Manatt, Phelps & Phillips. Mr. Grossman focuses on tax, corporate, transactional and regulatory matters. He is involved in the development and organization of integrated health delivery systems including regional community health networks, nonprofit medical foundations, physician-hospital organizations, management/administrative services organizations and other entities aimed at integrating physicians, hospital and other providers and suppliers of health care services in a managed care environment. Mr. Grossman received a B.A. in Political Science from the University of California, Los Angeles, a J.D. from the School of Law, Southwestern University, Los Angeles, CA, and a Master of Law in Taxation from Georgetown University Law Center, Washington, D.C.

JEFFREY S. PION

Jeffrey S. Pion is First Vice President and member of CB Commercial's Healthcare Group. Before joining CB Commercial, Mr. Pion was vice president of a real estate investment and development organization. He graduated from Punahou School in Honolulu, Hawaii and received a degree in Economics form the University of California, Santa Barbara.

ERIC A. TUCKMAN

Mr. Tuckman is Vice President/General Counsel and Asst. Secretary for Centinela Hospital Medical Center. He is a member of the senior management team of a $200 MM diversified healthcare company. Mr. Tuckman's specific responsibilities include the evaluation, development and transactional implementation of new business ventures. He received a B.A. from the State University of New York at Binghamton and a J.D. from the School of Law, University of Pittsburgh.

GPSR Compliance

The European Union's (EU) General Product Safety Regulation (GPSR) is a set of rules that requires consumer products to be safe and our obligations to ensure this.

If you have any concerns about our products, you can contact us on ProductSafety@springernature.com

In case Publisher is established outside the EU, the EU authorized representative is:

Springer Nature Customer Service Center GmbH
Europaplatz 3
69115 Heidelberg, Germany

Batch number: 10837190

Printed by Printforce, the Netherlands